Isaac Bobin

Letters of Isaac Bobin

Isaac Bobin

Letters of Isaac Bobin

ISBN/EAN: 9783337247812

Printed in Europe, USA, Canada, Australia, Japan

Cover: Foto ©ninafisch / pixelio.de

More available books at **www.hansebooks.com**

New York Colonial Tracts.

Number IV.

𝕷𝖊𝖙𝖙𝖊𝖗𝖘 𝖔𝖋 𝕴𝖘𝖆𝖆𝖈 𝕭𝖔𝖇𝖎𝖓,

LETTERS

OF

Isaac Bobin, Esq.,

PRIVATE SECRETARY OF

HON. GEORGE CLARKE,

Secretary of the Province of New York.

1718-1730.

ALBANY, N. Y.:
J. MUNSELL, 82 STATE ST.
1872.

LETTERS

OF

ISAAC BOBIN.

Anthony Barry to Ifaac Bobin.

LONDON, *Auguft ye* 4th 1718.

My Dear Bobin

I HAD the favour of both Your's of the 20th of November and 31ſt of May, which were not a little welcome to me, the latter I got but Yeſterday. Though I was not at *Dublin* when the firſt came, I delayed but little time till I ſent your friends

A

there the fubftance of it, which I
am perfwaded they were glad to
fee.   I am heartily concerned at the
melancholy Story of your Voyage but
fince it's over, cannot but congratulate You on your Arrival and the
kind reception You have mett with
from Your Relation there, & hope
you will e'er long reap the benefit
of Your going.

Warner was mightily difappointed
of having a Commiffion in *Wade's*
Regiment, which is fince *Hawley's*,
for the prefent Colonel is a Man
little beloved, and One of a very
odd Temper, however by chance
he got One in Brigadier *Borr's*
Regim^t of Marines, to be a Second
Lieutenant, which is only Enfign's
Pay, they laid at *Gallway* when
We left *Ireland;* I cannot but take
notice to You, that for Some time
before he got it, he was at a Lofs

for Your Affiftance to help him out
with a Memorial now and then to
My Lord Lieut: which out of a
friendfhip to You (he being one as
you refpected) I did with a great
deal of Pleafure, but when he got
his Bufinefs done, and was commanded to Quarters, did not fo
much as thank me or take his leave
of me, or any other of Your friends
ab^t the Office.

I came to *London* in April laft
(and as Sudden as We came before)
with Mr. *Budgell* he is very kind
to me & I doubt not but will be
my very good Patron[1] I did (as
you defired) prefent Your humble
Refpects to him, which he took
very kindly & afked heartily after
you. Monf^r *Duranc* is with us &
gives his kind Service to You.

We had great Alteration in the
Secretary's Office fince You left this

Country, for when the Duke of
Bolton was there, Mr. *Towers* was
ill of a fever about thirteen weeks,
and was Several times thought paſt
recovery, during which time I offi-
ciated in the Office for him, and
when he recovered he left it and
came hither, at which time Mr.
Budgell put me into the Office at
£30 ℔ Annum, where I continued
about a Quarter, and then he coming
to *London* brought me with him ;
Since Our being here Mr. *Webſter*
(Chief Sec^ry to the Duke of *Bolton*)
have inſtead of Mr. *William Budgell's*
acting as Secry to the Lords Juſtices,
appointed Mr. *Maddocks* (a friend
of his) to act, and Sent Over a Young
Gentleman from hence to be in
my Place in the Office ; Notwith-
ſtanding this, I doubt not, but Mr.
Budgell will in a ſhort time out top
Webſter and all other his Adverſaries.

Betty Lovell fhould have been Marryed to One Mr. *Wallett* (whom you have often heard her Name) in January laft, nay fhe reported herfelf that She was So, and went by the Name for fome time, but whatever the matter was, the Match was fpoil'd, She broke off with him, and was abfent for about two months that neither her Mother nor Sifters knew where She was, and Juft as We came to *London*, She came to Light again, and is lately marryed to One Mr. *Vanderhagen* a Land-fkip Drawer, with whom She lives very happily, he is a very fober man, a handfome man and a good huf-band, So I think after all fhe may be thankfull to her ftars.

Mr. *Elliot* is out of Bufinefs, and where I can't tell, for I have not feen him thefe two Months, but if I do fhall Shew him thofe Parts of Your Letters that mention him.

I wrote to Mr. *Heath* about the Hats You mention in Your former Letter for him to Send you, but never received a Line from him relating to them, waiting for which, was the occafion I did not anfwer it fooner, but fince Yours of the 31ft of May came before I anfwered the other, I hope you will excufe my anfwering them both in One, which I am afraid will tire Your Patience in perufing, but fince it is but feldom, that an Opportunity Serve for Our hearing from One another, I am perfwaded You will pafs by that fault; And I do affure You, it is my hearty Defire, that We may keep up a Conftant Correfpondence, and that as often as poffible.

Billy Dowell is married to a Young Woman that was a By Blow of My Lord *Southwell's*, One of the Commiffioners of the Revenue in *Ireland*,

who when You were there was only
Sir *Thomas Southwell*, I believe My
Lord gave him £3 or 400 and I
fancy will put him in fome Em-
ployment in the Cuftom houfe.

I am at a great Lofs here for
want of Your Company, which
would very much add to my Satif-
faction, but when I confider the
advantage Your abfence from hence
will be of to You I content Myfelf
in fome meafure & recommend You
to the care of the Omnipotent. I
am

Dear Bobin
Your fincere friend
& humble Servt
ANTHONY BARRY.

P. S. Since my writing this Epiftle,
Mr. *Budgell* has defired me particu-
larly to give his Service to You which
is a Sign that You are in his fav^r.

I defire you would continue Your Directions to me under Mr. *Belcher's* Cover.

The *D:* of *Bolton* is ftill Ld Lieu^t & the talk about y^e *D:* of *Newcaftle* is over.

Ifaac Bobin to George Clarke.

Long Island, O&r 4th 1718.

Hon^d Sir.

I HAVE paid Mr. *Barberie* The two Warrants for which I have taken the inclof'd receipt.

My prefumption in going abroad too foon has been the Motive of my often thinking of what yor honour told me; I fhall take care for the future not to be fo bold.

My long abfence from the Office makes me very uneafy, But hope in a few days to be able to attend

it, I'm brought low my diſtemper
having been very ſevere. My hand
is ſo weak that I cant be ſo prolix
as I could wiſh to expreſs the ſence
of my duty as I ought to him who
I hope will do me the Juſtice to
believe that I am
   Hon^d Sir
      Your dutifull
       and moſt
        Obedient humble
        Servant
         I. Bobin.
To *George Clark* Eſq.

Iſaac Bobin to George Clarke.

New York, Secretary's Office,
Febry the 6th, 171⅞.

Hon^d Sir

UPON Receipt of yor Letter of
the 28th of Janry laſt I went
to Mr. *Wileman* and in regard to

B

Yo^r Inftructions preff'd him for Yo^r Acco^{ts} who gives his Service to you and beggs yor farther patience for they fhall be ready in a few days I fhall not let often calling for 'em be wanting, and fo foon as they come to my hands fend 'em you.

I fent yor Letter to Mr. *Alexander* at *Amboy* where he is with the Governour, and dont expeſt him home before the Latter End of this Month or beginning of next. In Obedience to Yo^r Commands is Inclofed yor Quarterly Warrants wch till now I had not an Oppertunity to fend.

As to Yo^r Office you need not be afraid it fhall fuffer either prejudice or delay, it will not Appear that ever I have been negligent in doing my duty or that ever I made a flight of bufinefs relating thereto on the

(**11**)

Contrary have not nor fhall be
wanting in my Endeavours to keep
bufinefs fo that it run not behind
hand, Neverthelefs meet with fmall
Encouragement, Mr. *Alexander* lay-
ing Claim to the little Perquifites
I make of the marryage Lycences,
but don't doubt you'll fet that matter right (when you come to Town)
it being fo unreafonable and as I'm
informed what has never been prac-
ticed by his Predeceffors and wch if
he keeps cant propofe to go the
Circuits and to fubfift on a Stipend
of twenty pounds ℔ Ann. The
Perfon that inform'd you I was at
my Uncles thofe days you mention
is under a miftake and hope you'll
do me the Juftice to believe it as
fuch And that I am with great
truth and Refpect

S^r

Yours &c.

I. Bobin.

Isaac Bobin to George Clarke.

NEW YORK, SECRETARY'S OFFICE,
February the 16th 171⅞.

Hon^d Sir.

BEING Apprehenfive of your fear of the Small Pox in your family, have prefumed to fend the enclofed Remedy of Dr *Samuell Wilday* which I hope will meet with your honour's kind acceptance (which if it does will anfwer my wifh) having nothing more at heart than the welfare of your honour and family, being with great truth and Refpect.

Sir

Your moft humble
and moft obed^t Servant
I. BOBIN.

I hear from *Amboy* that the Govr is recover'd from his late Indifpofition.

Isaac Bobin to George Clarke.

New York, Secretary's Office,
November the 17th 1719.

Hon^d Sir.

INCLOSED is the Act of Assem-
bly (wch I take by the Purport
of your Letter to be the Act you
want) had your Letters come sooner
to hand your Commands had been
obey'd before this But flatter myself
you'll do me the Justice not to
believe any omission on my side, or
that my diligence has been wanting
to forward what you so Earnestly
desired, I have sent by *Will* all the
other matters you Requested, Ex-
cepting Oat meal wch was not to be
got in Town   As to Beer Cyder
&c^a Mr. *Schuyler* tells me he hopes
to send the Latter End of this week,
as Mr. *Schuyler* has sent you a Letter

to day, *Will* dont doubt but he has ſatiſſyed you as to that therefore believe I need ſay no more on that Head.

Iſaac Bobin to George Clarke.

Jany 2ᵈ 1719.

Hon. Sir

I MAKE uſe of this opportunity to Congratulate you your good Spouſe and Madᵐ *Hyde* on the New Year ardently wiſhing it may be followed by many others in health proſperity and pleaſure — having nothing more at Heart than the welfare of your Honour and family.

The preſident tells me he has received a Letter from Coll. *Rutſen* wherein he mentioned the Receipt of the Patent and that he ſhall be here in the Spring and make all matters eaſy on that ſcore.

I ſend herewith according to your
Orders by Mr. *Nicolls* 1 pˢ Brown
Ozanbrigs qᵗ 55 Ells at 18ᴰ Dᵒ
Broad Garlix Nᵒ 33 £4 5 12
pound of Nails Six pound Double
tens and Six pound of Single tens
at 10ſ ¼d ₱ pound 2 Oz of Parſely
ſeed 1 Ounce of Cabbage Lettice
ſeed As to Onion, Garden Beans
and Savory ſeed I cant get but ſhall
make farther Enquiry and ſend by
the firſt opportunity.

Mr. *Schuyler* will uſe his Utmoſt
Endeavour in getting of Oats as
mentioned in your Letter. He tells
me has been ſeveral times with
Mr. *Hooper* for that Money and as
urgent as poſſible, but has not as yet
received it but ſo ſoon as it comes
to his hands ſhall pay it where you
were pleaſed to order it.

I ſhall as you are pleaſed to Command me call often on Mr. *Wileman*

for your Accounts but as the Xmas
is not yet over

Capt *Goelet* arrived this day from
Amfterdam after a long Paffage of
Sixteen Weekes but has as I can learn
brought no News worth your Judi-
cious Obfervation, therefore fhall
conclude as I really am with all
due Refpect.

Ifaac Bobin to George Clarke.

Jany 21st 1719.

S^r

I RECEIVED yours of the 14th
Inft to day, as to what you hint
relating to the Patent I fhall not
be remifs in obferving Capt *Jarrate*
has made his Return of Survey and
to Day was brought by Mr. *Sharpas*
to the Office with a Petition in
Order to be laid before the Council,

but have not had any fince the 24th
of Decr laft, The prefident having
been Indifpof'd but tells me he
defigns to call a Council to morrow,
So foon as prefent I will take care
to Execute your Commands.

it being late when yours came to
hand and the bearer in hafte had
not time to get a Pen knife, therefore have fent you mine, wch I hope
you will find fit for your purpofe —
As to the reft mentioned I fhall ufe
my utmoft Endeavour in getting
them as foon as poffible.

Ifaac Bobin to George Clarke.

S^r

I RECEIVED yours of ye 1st Inftant by the hands of Monf^r
Fauconnier, and in regard thereto
have promifed to let him have fome

C

moneys by the latter End of next Week, hoping by that time to raife fuch a fume as may anfwer yours and his Expectations upon wᶜʰ hee feemed fatisfyed I fhall not be wanting to ufe my utmoft Endeavour and diligence in perfecting the fame.

The Moneys now in my hand being fmall could not conceive it would be of any fervice to offer him any at this Juncture, was the motive of my Referring it till the time as before Expreffed.

I have likewife received yours of the 3ᵈ inft. and fend herewith 4 doz of Coat Buttons at 4∫ ₴ doz & Dᵒ of Waft Coat at 2∫ being the fmalleft and beft I could get, as alfo two Doe fkins at 6∫ each 12 pound of Chocolate at 20∫ and two Pack of Cards 3∫ it being late in the Day and the Weather bad when I received yours had not time to get the feeds, but do defign to fend 'em by the next Convenience wth the five Bufhells of peas you wrote for, wch I doubt not but you'll find good. As to Garden Beans I have been feveral Places and can't meet wth any yet but fhall make further Inquiry.

As to the Children's Cloaths, your Servant as fhould have been the bearer of y^r letter not coming near me, but fending it by *Will*, my Hands were tyed as to that affair, but having rec^d a note from Mrs. *Ludlow* fignifying her want of money to be neceffary, for that purpofe, fent in Anfwer that I was forry I could not Comply wth her requeft, but that if fhe would buy the things fhe wanted I would take care the money fhould be paid upon wch fhe feemed affronted, Neverthelefs offered to buy them myfelf

provided fhe would let me know
what fhe wanted, but I was not
worthy an anfwer.

I fend inclofed your Pen knife
wch I got mended by the man near
the Wind Mill.

Yo^r Patent met with no obftruc-
tion and is near compleated, it being
now Ingrofeing and will fo foon as
paft the feal obferve your directions
relating thereto.

I am

Yours &c.

I. B.

February ye 3^d 1719.

The Veffell for *London* is not yet
failed, But 'tis thought will by the
End of this week.

Isaac Bobin to George Clarke.

NEW YORK, SECRETARY's OFFICE,
June the 17*th* 1720.

Hon^d Sir.

I RECEIVED yours of the 15th by *Riche* this morning, I send by him, Wine, Rum, Canary and what else you were pleased to order. Sir, *Riche* being in haste and the Councill going to sett, has prevented my design in Sending you an Acc^t of the particulars I sent by him the last Trip.

I shall use my utmost Dilligence in getting what money I can, and shall observe what you tell me concerning your Warrants which are not as yet signed but will be to Day.

As to News there is very little, Capt *Smith* is fallen down to the

Watering Place in order to ſaile for *London* in the afternoone, I paid him two Guineas and took his Receipt wᶜʰ I incloſ'd in Mr. *Worſams* as you Directed and put it in the Bagg at Mr. *Sharpas's* together with the reſt of yoʳ Letters. Capᵗ *Pearce* upon ſome words ariſing between him and his Lieut. has ſuſpended him and Confin'd him in his Cabbin.

Coll. *Rutſen* has been in Town, and tho' I had not received your Letter before his Departure, I acquainted him of the ill Conſequences that might attend his Delaying to have the Patent of *Hurly* Compleated, the Preſident did the like upon which he promiſed to wait on me at the Office in order to ſettle that affair but has left the Town without coming near me I believe the occaſion of it is the want of Money.

I have not received your Fees for the Patent of *Cornelius Low* altho' I am as prefling as poffible.

Capt. *Ouvery* is dayly Expected from *London*.

I hope agriculture and Horticulture thrive.   I am &c

Yours

I. BOBIN.

George Clarke Efq^r

Edward Hyde to Ifaac Bobin.

Dear Mr. *Bobin*

I HAVE fent ye Taylor to you and beg ye favor that you will fend Mr. *Reynolds* for to Buy fome Cloath pray let it not be Coarfe, I fhall be at your Office to morrow and Excufe this from

Your moft

humble Servt

EDW^D HYDE.

Friday 1 Clock.

pray send me word if Mr. *Clarke*
as sent down my Bill

Isaac Bobin to George Clarke.

June ye 24th 1720.

Sir

I HAVE received yours of the
20th by *Riche*, and send herewith by him what you tell me
was wanting vizt 34 & ½ Gallons of
Molasses at 2ƒ p^r Gallon, three
Gallons of Whale Oyle at 4ƒ ℔
Gallon wch being scarce was all I
could get. 3. Bushells of Salt at
3ƒ & 6d ℔ Bushell a piece of striped
Silk Muslin at 5d bought at Mr.
Franks.

As to Beef Mr. *Schuyler* promised
me he would take care to send
by this opportunity therefore dont
doubt but he'll give you an acc^t.

Mr. *Gathehoufe* prefents you his humble Duty, and defired me to acquaint you that he'll go about makeing more garden fticks and is very glad you like thofe he has fent, but is forry that he forgot to Pitch the Bottoms to prevent there rotting but fhall take care to do it to next ftakes he makes I fhall obferve what you tell me Concerning fruit when Veffells Come in. Capt. *Ouvery* arrived here Yefterday after a Paffage of Ten Weeks from the *Lizard Point*. The Prefident receiv'd a letter from Brigd^r *Hunter* dat. 26th of March laft, in wch he informs him as he did in his former that he is perfectly recovered of his late Indifpofition, and that he hopes to be here foon, but can't be punctual as to what time he fhall take his Departure his private and Publick affairs taking up fo

D

much of his time — this is the purport of his Letter as the Prefident
tells me.

Capt. *Ouvery* Reports that Mr.
Burnet is appointed Govr of this
Province but what grounds he has
for the news can't tell.

I fend inclofed two Letters w^ch
Mr. *Sharpas* gave me this Morning
to forward to You I gave yor Letters to him for *Bofton*. Wednefday
laft a foldier belonging to Coll.
Weems Compa. was drowned in the
North River, by going to his Canoe
wch was afloat by the Rifing of the
Tide, he was hardly got up to his
Sholders before he Sunck, Some
believe he was hurt by a Shark —
others that it was the

Iſaac Bobin to George Clarke.

N. Y., SECRY'S OFEICE,
July yᵉ 22d, 1720.

Honᵈ Sir

I HAVE receiv'd yours of the 16ᵗʰ by Mr. *Nicholls* I muſt Confeſs 'tis a Error my not ſending you an Accᵗ of the things I ſend by *Riche,* but for the future ſhall be punctuall in & obſerving your Directions therein & for yoʳ ſatisfaction ſend now an accᵗ of things I ſent by him laſt Trip & there prices as follows (vizᵗ) a Doz pd. of Chocolate 1℔ 2ſ 12 pound of ſoap 7ſ 8d 1 Sive 2ſ a Roap of Onions one Sh. 12pᵈ ſtarch & Bagg. 10ſ 6d 4 Bottles of Lime Juice 11ſ 2 Barrills Lamb Black 1ſ The Rum you mention I ſhall ſend by *Riche* with 200 of Limes I have not had 'em from

Mr. *Harrison* but got them from a
friend, and as often as I get any
will fend.

I fpoke to Mr. *Schuyler* concerning your Fire ftones being Broke,
who tells me he is certain that when
they were deliver'd to *Riche* they
were all whole but was apprehenfive
that fome accident would happen
to them in yᵉ unloading, he belive-
ing the Tackleing of his Boat was
not ftrong enough or fit for that
purpofe and gave him a Caution to
take care.

I received your Letter of the ——
by Mrs. *Grace Sewell*, I fend by her
a pʳ of filk ftockings at 19ſ 6 yards
of Calicoe 1ſ 6d a pʳ of Cizors 1ſ
Whale Bone 3 & to

Isaac Bobin to George Clarke.

NEW YORK, SECRETARY'S OFFICE,
July the 26th 1720.

Hon^d Sir

I RECEIVED your Letter of Yef-
terday p^r Mr. *Holland*, with not
a Little trouble and Concern to
perceive you fhould think yourfelf
impofed on by me in the charge or
price of things bought for you, I
fhould be very forry you fhould
fuffer any prejudice or injury on
that fcore or any other, if fo 'tis
not knowingly to me and is reverfe
to my inclination, I have been
obliged fome time, when my time
would not permit me to take a
Circuit through the Town to buy
things, and yor occafions for 'em
urgent, To Confide in *Reynolds* &

hope he has done me juftice, as to
what is mention'd in relation to
Chocolate it is not to be bought
und^r 22 ſ tho' I know as you remark
I have had it at Dugdales at 20 ſ
but he has not any left and if he
had could not afford it und^r Cocoa
being advanced in it's price—as to
Soap and Starch if I am impoſed
on they were bought at one Pel-
letrous near Mr. *Jordains*, When
you come to Town if you require
it the man ſhall be brought before
you to Clear that point. And as
to the other things I ſhall do the
like.

The Rum ſent by *Riche* is 12
Gallons and is by thoſe who pretend to underſtand it eſteem'd to be
very good, the price is 4 ſ ℔ Gallon
if it be not likt it it will be taken
again—I bought it upon y^t Condition.

According to yor ord^r I have paid
Mrs. *Stollard* 5 pound and taken
her receipt for the fame. I have
been with *Jofeph Latham* concerning the Note of Mr. *Nicholls* in
your favour, who tells me the
money is not due before the firft of
May next Neverthelefs if he had
money in his Hands woud advance
it which he will be ready to do as
foon as he has fold a fhip belonging
to him, and fays you may be affured
it fhall be the firft paid, but feems
to infift upon the reward promifed.
S^r I cannot conclude without beg-
ging leave to take notice of a Hint
in your Letter That among Trading
men I fhould be ill thought of. I
I can't tell how I might be Deemed
in the Eye of my Country But very
well know my Confcience void and
free from any Male-practices what-
foever fo that I can (if occafion be)

the better vindicate my Innocence
on that Head. I return you thanks
for your kind Cautions, wch I ſhall
obſerve and ſhall ever make it my
ſtudy to merit your good Opinion,
and hope you'll do me the Juſtice
to believe me to be as I really am
with the greateſt regard

Hon^d Sir
Yours &c
I. BOBIN.

I ſent by *Riche* Mr. *Hydes* Wigg
the price is 4ſ 10*d* he'll take it
again if not approved of at that
price.

To *George Clarke* Eſq^r

(33)

Iſaac Bobin to George Clarke.

NEW YORK, SECRETARY'S OFFICE,
July the 30th 1720.

Sʳ

I HAVE received this day your letter of Yeſterday, by *Will.*

As ſoon as it came to hand I went to Mr. *Hoopers* he was not at home I ſpoke to his ſpouſe upon yᵉ ſubject matter of yʳ letter relating to a Negro, ſhe tells me they have not any negro's to diſpoſe off, but expect ſome from the Weſt Indies every Day.

Mr. *Schuyler* is not in Town ſo can ſay no more at preſent on that Head but ſhall make Inquiry as you direct and let you know When I find one I think may ſuit you wᶜʰ I ſhall do without delay — As to what things Capt. *Smith* delivered me belonging (as he told me) to

E

Mr. *Hyde* were as follows (to wit) an Old p^r of Britches Weaſt Coat and Rugg The Rugg I made uſe of to Rap the Burois(?) and other things I ſent to the *Plains,* ſome time ago ℔ *Cæſar;* the other I have put in a obſcure place in the Office.

I ſhall be punɗuall in taking notice of your Commands concerning Mr. *Burnets* arrival here and will not be wanting to forward an Expreſs ſo ſoon as I hear of his approach.

I will Endeavour to manage the beſt I can with *Jos. Latham.*

Capt *Moulton* 'tis thought will ſaile for *London* the Latter end of next week.

I ſend herewith a p^r of gray Stockings at 10ſ which I hope will fit, if not may be returned, and ſhall for the future buy nothing but

upon that Condition, ſo yᵗ if you
ſhould think I am impoſed on in
the prices know what to do, but
will Endeavour to prevent if poſſible
that trouble.

There's no news in Town but
Our Dayly Expeᶜtation of Mr.
Burnet, and have nothing more to
add but my hearty wiſhes for the
health and proſperity of your Family
Being with all Due Reſpeᶜt
Sir &c.
I. Bobin.

Geo Clarke Eſqʳ.

Iſaac Bobin to George Clarke.

N. York, *Augᵗ* 2ᵈ 1720.

Honᵈ Sir.

I RECEIVED to day your Letter
of Yeſterday by the Hands of
Brazier, I have been wᵗʰ Capᵗ *Van-*

brugh who arrived here on Sunday
laſt from *Barbadoes*, he has brought
wth him four Negroes, two Men &
two Women, but has only a man
he can recommend as a real good
ſlave, and believes will ſuit you, he
underſtands Cookery, and knows
how to wait at Table, and in all
manner of Houſehold Affairs is no
ſtranger, he is a Luſty Negro aged
about 30 years, has lived with a
Gent. in *Barbados* who falling under
unhappy Circumſtances was obliged
to ſell him, but not for any miſde-
meanour he ever Committed, The
loweſt price he tells me is 55 pounds
ready money—otherwiſe will not
diſpoſe of him—as to ſending the
Negro up in the Country upon
Tryall he ſeem not willing, but is
ready to leave him at any Gent^s
Houſe in Town as you think your
friend upon liking for 7 or 8 days,

and defires your anfwer as foon as
poffible.

Simon the Jew dont expect his
fhip from *Guinea* before late in the
fall

The Paper I mentioned to you
was by miftake left behind but fhall
fend it with the Chequered Linen
by *Riche*.

Ifaac Bobin to George Clarke.

NEW YORK, SECRETARY'S OFFICE,
Augt the 6th, 1720.

S^r

I SEND by *Riche* a Barrell of
Porke at three pounds two and
fix pence it being fcarce could not
get it under, the Man I bought it
off was Mr. *Painter'd* who warrants
it to be good Mr. *Jonneau* had not
any he could recomend 11⅜ yard
Checquer'd Linen at 3ƒ £1. 14. 10⅜

12 Gallons of Molaſſes at 2ſ; a Buſhel of Peas at 6ſ. I have paid *Dirk Mott* 3 pound fifteen ſhillings, and by whom I have ſent 2 doz. and a half of Limes and 1 qʳ of fine Paper & 2 of Courſe.

I hope you received my Letter concerning the Negro.

Sʳ I beg you'll excuſe my Brevity the Councill juſt a going to ſett and *Riche* in haſte, The Preſident will go for *Albany* Tueſday next, Capt. *Moulton* will Saile for London the Latter End of next Week.

I am &c.

I. Bobin.

George Clarke Eſq.

Isaac Bobin to George Clarke.

NEW YORK, SECRETARY'S OFFICE,
August the 11th 1720.

Hon^d Sir

I RECEIVED Yesterday by *Riche* your Letter of the 8th instant, by which I find the Negro of Capt *Vanbrugh* will not suit for am told as to matters belonging to the field he is a stranger having been intirely brought up to affairs of the house so have let that Drop, Mr. *Schuyler* who is come to Town jnforming me that Vessells are dayly expected from the West Indies with Negros, and shall not be slack in useing his utmost Endeavours to get one he thinks may suit your purpose, therefore beggs your patience till then.

The President designs to go for *Albany* to morrow morning.   His

Majefties Ship *Kinfale* is fallen down
to the Wattering Place in order to
Saile for Great Britain. Capt *Moulton* will faile very Speedyly for
London.

Ifaac Bobin to George Clarke.

Auguft 22^d 1720.

Hon^d Sir

I HAVE received your Letters of
the 13th and 18th jnftant, I fend
now by *Riche* a Canifter of Bohea
Tea at £1 14ʃ Candles the like
Quantity as before, Cloves ¼ of a
Pound at 7ʃ a Sive or Ridle for
lime at 2ʃ 3*d* & a piece of Diaper
12 Yards £1 14ʃ. I could not find
any in Town of a greater Quantity
to the p^s except at Mr. *Barberies*
where I found Lawn of 60 Yards

to the p^s but Believed that would
not fuit if this I have fent fhou'd
not be likt it will be taken again, I
could not find any Garlick in Town,
As to a Negro Mr. *Schuyler* and I
Wee have ufed Our utmoft Endeavour to get one, Capt *Hopkins* has
one to difpofe off but Mr. *Schuyler*
thought him off too high a price
being 50 pounds the loweft and
would not let go from his houfe on
Tryall So muft have patience till
Veffells come in I could not per-
fwade *V. Brugh* to fend his Negro
to the *Plains* I have delivered Your
Letters to Mr. *Fauconnier* and Mr.
Sharpas and p^d *Blake* five pound as
ordered &

I am yours
I. BOBIN.

To *George Clarke.*

F

Isaac Bobin to George Clarke.

Aug* 29*th* 1720.

Hon^d Sir.

I HAVE received your Letter of the 26th jnftant by the Hands of Mr. *Nicholls* and am glad to hear the Diaper I fent was well liked but on the other Hand forry it was not the fort Mad^m *Clarke* intended. *James Martin* has been with me with the Note you mention, I have promifed to pay it when due upon which one Afhton in Town has given him credit for Leather, he was at Mr. *Schuylers* but did not find any Leather there to fuit his purpofe.

As to the Note drawn in favour of *Jordain* Capt. *Walton* upon *Jordains* Endorfing it has accepted it from him as Cafh and is very well fatisfyed with payment thereof in Eight or tenn Days.

I fhall obferve what you tell me concerning the Sallary Warrants and will Endeavour if poffible to finifh with the Lawyers, but have no hopes of Compleating matters with thofe Gents I have writt to Coll *Rutfon* informing him of the ill Confequence of leaving the Patent of *Hurley* un Recorded &c^a but have not heard from him fince I will take care of Returning the Lottery Ticketts, and the delivery of yor Letter to Coll *Heathcote* as likewife to fend by *Rich* the things by you ordered

To Mr. *Clarke*.

Isaac Bobin to George Clarke.

NEW YORK, *August* 31*st* 1720.

Sr

I SEND by *Riche* 3 Bushells of
Salt at 3 ʃ and 6*d* ℔, 6 yards of
Ozinbriggs 8 ʃ, 4 Ropes of Onions
4 ʃ ¼ ℔ Nutmegs 6 ʃ Garlick which
I got of a French Man from *New
Rochell* there is little above a pound.
I hope Mr. *Nicholls* has acquainted
you that I have paid him 10 ʃ above
what was ordered in your Laſt, I
was backward in doing it but as he
preſt me to ſtretch a point dont
doubt but he will do me the Juſtice
to tell you of the ſame.

I ſhall ſend you in my next an
Account of what money I have paid
him, there is no News in Town
ſince my Laſt, I am with Reſpeςt
&c.

IS BOBIN.

To Mr Secry *Clarke.*

Isaac Bobin to George Clarke.

NEW YORK, *Sept. 6th* 1720.

Hon^d Sir

SINCE my laſt to you of Yeſterday I have received Yours of
2^d ℔ *Riche*, that wch came Incloſed
I after Reading & Sealing Delivered
as Directed. Mr. *Janſen* has given
me the Patent of *Hurly* in order to
be Recorded, and tells me that by
the firſt opportunity he ll write to
Coll *Rutſen* to haſten him to Town
ſo that matters relating to y^t affair
may be compleated and every thing
made Eaſy on that ſcore I will take
Care to obſerve the Caution you
give me touching the ſaid Patent,
as I ſhall always do the like in
every thing elſe that may be hinted,
I ſend now by *Riche* 6¼ ℔ of New
Tarr'd Rope inch & ½ at 7½*d* being
ten Fathom bought at Mr. *Dugdales*,

As to *Albany* ſtale Beer I cant get
any in Town, ſo was obliged to go
to *Rutgers* where I found none Older
than Eight Days I was backward in
ſending ſuch but *Riche* telling me
you wanted Beer for your workmen
and did not know what to do without have run the hazard to ſend two
Barr^ls at £1 16ſ. the Barr^ls at 3ſ. ℔
p^s 6ſ. *Rutgers* ſays it is extraordinary good Beer and y^t racking it
off into other Barr^ls wou'd flatten it
and make it Drink Dead, I ſhall
not inlarge any more on this Head
by reaſon *Riche* will inform you
further what was ſay'd and am with
all due Regard.

S^r

&c

ISAAC BOBIN.

To Mr. *Clarke.*

(47)

Iſaac Bobin to George Clarke.

NEW YORK, SECRY'S OFFICE,
Sept. 7ᵗʰ 1720.

Honᵈ Sir

COLL *Heathcote* deſired me to forward the incloſed and gave me a note of thirteen pounds drawn on Mr. *Van Dam* in your favour which he paid upon Sight You have herewith likewiſe an accᵗ of the Ship *Swanſwick*, and as Wee have no News in Town but what the American *Weekly Mercury* from *Philadelphia* tells us, I flatter myſelf my ſending one by this Opportunity will meet with your kind acceptance wᶜʰ that it may will be the ardent wiſh of him who's with Reſpect &c.

Isᶜ BOBIN.

I have not ſucceeded with the Lawyers.

To Mr. *Clarke.*

(48)

Iſaac Bobin to George Clarke.

NEW YORK, SECRETARY'S OFFICE,
Novr the 15th 1720.

Hon^d Sir

I SEND now by *Riche* the ſeveral particulars mention'd in your Letter of the 5th and 10th jnſt. except Braſs Buttons wch are not to be found in Town; incloſed is an account of the Coſt of Mr. *Hyde's* Clothes Trimming &c^a The Aſſembly its thought will break up Friday or Saturday next, I begg S^r you'll excuſe my Brevity my time not permiting to mention ye particulars of what I ſend. I will be Watchfull and Carefull in all things being with all due regard.

Hon^d S^r
&c.

Edward Hyde to Iſaac Bobin.

Novr 23^d 1720.

Sir

BY ye bearer hereof—I beg you
will pay Six Shillings. I ſhall
be down this week or next week
foredeſt Captⁿ *Pevice* as ſent for me
to Repair on board, I ſhall pay
you when I am down and ſhall take
it allwayes as an obligation done to
your freind and

humble Servant

EDW^D HYDE.

Elinoar Arnell ye Bearer.

G

Ifaac Bobin to George Clarke.

New York, Secretary's Office,
*December y*e* 17*th* 1720.

Hon^d Sir.

I SEND now by *Riche* a Loaf of Suguar Seven pound and a q^r @ 2*ſ* ℔ pound, bought at Mr. *Loyds,* I have been at the Shoemakers for Mad^m *Clarke's* Shoes who tells me they'll not be finiſhed before Tueſday next, I have been likewiſe with *Sonmine* for Mad^m *Hyde* and Miſs *Molly's* Thimbls, they are not yet compleated but am promiſed them on Monday next without fail. I flatter myſelf Mad^m *Hyde* will not think my often calling for her Thimble and Miſs *Molly's* has been wanting. I have not as yet the forty pound in hand but expeét to raiſe that ſum by Wedneſday or

Thurſday next. Mr. *Byerly* cannot
help me having been diſappointed
of money promiſed him on account
of the Quit Rents—Neverthelefs
don't doubt to ſucceed otherways.

I hear Mr. *Hyde* has not been on
ſhoar ſince you left the Town being
confin'd on Board.

I hope the Roots &c may prove
to content, and that agriculture and
Horticulture may thrive mainly at
the *Plains*, where I wiſh you, Mad^m
Clarke, Mad^m *Hyde* and Little
Famyly health proſperity and pleaſure being very ſincerely

Isaac Bobin to George Clarke.

SECRY'S OFFICE, NEW YORK,
Jany 4th 172⁰/₁.

Hond Sir,

YOURS of the 30th of Decr laft came to hand the 31st of the fame Inftant the Letter you fent inclofed I delivered to his Excellency who has not as yet given me any directions concerning the Commiffions of appraziers &ca the many and frequent vifits made him fince the Holydays has not permitted him to confider of the fame. I will as foon as I have his orders difpatch thofe for yor County; inclofed is a Coppy of *John Bridges* Comm. to be Surrogate I have been with Coll *Depeyfter* in order to know when his accounts will be ready to be audited, who tells me he has not as

yet made any progreſs to that End,
but deſigns to make a Beginning in
a few Days,   The time when they'll
be Compleated cannot ſay.   The
Coll. ſeems under great concern.

I have received twenty four pounds
thirteen Shillings of Mr. *Byerly*, wᶜʰ
Sume I now ſend you by Mr. *Nicholls*.

As to marble Tiles or   there
is none in Town   Mr. *Cuyler* had
ſome but

Iſaac Bobin to Michael Kearney.

NEW YORK, SECRETARY's OFFICE,
January the 3ᵈ 172⁹⁄₈.

Sʳ

HIS Excellency commanded me
to ſend you the Encloſed Proclamations and to ſignifye that the
ſame Be Publiſhed in the uſuall
manner without Delay, and further

that you forthwith fend Circular
Letters to the Sev^l members of the
Affembly accquainting them that
his Excellency will be punctual in
meeting them purfuant to the time
mentioned in the faid Proclamations.
I have nothing more to add but that
I wifh you a happy New Year and
am with Refpect
> Your moft Obedient
> > humble Servant
> > > Is: BOBIN.

Michael Kearney Efq.

Ifaac Bobin to Lewis Morris.

SECRETARY'S OFFICE, NEW YORK,
Janry 5th 172⅘.

Hon^d Sir

YESTERDAY in Collecting
fome Papers here for the file,
the Ordinance for fiting of the

Supream Courts of Judicature &cᵃ
which Reviv'd that in the Brigadier's time to the firſt of December
laſt, came to Hand whereupon I
had the ſuggeſtion for its Revival;
I therefore take leave humbly to
give yoʳ Honour the intimation that
you'll pleaſe to conſider if it be of
importance, that Courſe be taken for
the continuance wᶜʰ your Honour
can only well conceive what is ap-
poſite to that purpoſe, with this and
wiſhing your Honour a proſperous
New Year I add that I am with all
poſſible Regards.
      Sir
        Your Honours
          Moſt humble and
            Moſt Obedᵗ Servant
               I. B.

Lewis Morris Eſqʳ Moriſania.

Isaac Bobin to George Clarke.

NEW YORK, SECRETARY's OFFICE,

*January y*ᵉ 18ᵗʰ 172⅞.

Honᵈ Sir

I RECEIVED yours of the 13ᵗʰ Current Saturday noon laſt and that Day ſent over, as you directed, particulars as in the encloſed. Since I have met wᵗʰ a pˢ of ſheeting *Holland* wᶜʰ I hope will prove to liking it contains — Ells at —— and now gos under the Care of Mr. *Nicholls* as well to be ſuppoſed yᵉ other mentioned things

What of Novelty occurred is that the Royal Prince Gally, Capᵗ *Payton*, from *Amſterdam* & *Cowes* in nine Weeks Paſſage from the latter is arrived by whom is Advice that S. Sea Stock has bin ruinous to many in *England* and *Holland*, it being

200 at that Veſſels departure and would as beleeved then realy fall under the Par: To particularize on one of the Diſtreſſed is that S^r *Joſ. Beck*, an Eminent Mercht, was quite bancrupt thereby. I have heard of a poetical fimile upon the Fall of this Stock In wch thoſe wch fucceeded therein are compared to *Moſes* paſſing the *Red Sea*, and thoſe unſuccesful nick't in the Rear to *Pharaoh's* Immerſion which followed. That Yatchs & Men of War were getting ready to attend His Majeſties Return And that there was a probability of Peace to be concluded with *Spain*.

H

Isaac Bobin to George Clarke.

NEW YORK, SECRETARY'S OFFICE,

Janry yͤ 26th 172⁸⁄₇.

Hon^d Sir

HIS Excellency defired me to
acquaint you That he has
had the affair of Appraiziers &c for
fome time under his Confideration
Yet cannot give Directions, or come
to any Refolution relating thereto
untill he fees you to difcourfe upon
the fubject matter of the Same.

In anfwer to yoͬ Letters of the
21st and 25th Inftant, I have been
with Mr. *Wileman* who tells me
that Mr. *Schuyler* has Executed the
Deeds for your Land. Mr. *Gate-
houfe* tells me he will get ready by
Eafter the Pine apples for the Top
of yoͬ Houfe as likewife the Garden
Sticks, he knows not of any perfon

for the purpofe you mention. I
have fpoke to Monſ^r *Fauconnier*
concerning a French young man
who will make it his bufineſs to
find one he thinks may be more to
your fatisfaction, and let me know
thereof. I ſhall obferve what you
write me concerning Bricks.

I have p^d *Blake* 40ſ according to
order and promifed Payment of the
£10 by the time Limited in yor
Note Drawn in his favour, which I
hope to perform tho' bufineſs in
the Office is not fo brifk as I could
wiſh.

I am glad Mad^m *Clarke* upon
opening the Linen likt it, It coſt
no more than 4ſ7½ an Englifh Ell,
and bought it upon Condition if not
approv'd of to be taken back.

I fend by *Blake* Parfely feed and
Sellery feed.

The Govr propofes to meet the

Affembly of yᵉ Jerfeys at *Burlington*
the Twentyfirſt of February next,
I dont hear what time he defigns
to go from hence — but as foon as
I do ſhall let you know.

I am &cᵃ

Is Bobin.

To *George Clarke* Efq.

Ifaac Bobin to George Clarke.

N. York, Secretary's Office,

February yᵉ 4ᵗʰ 172⁰⁄₇.

Hon Sir

ACCORDING to direction in
yoʳ Letter of Yeſterday, I been
at Mr. *Wileman's* for the Deeds
Mr. *Schuyler* has Executed, but did
not fee him by reafon of his being
much indifpofed with the Gout. I
ſhall call there again and as foon as
they come to hand get Mr. *Schuyler*

to acknowledge them and then
Record them. I have been likewife with Coll *Depeyfter* who tells
he has made a ftep towards Compleating his Acc^{ts} but can't fay when
they'll be ready to be auditted.

I fend now by Mr. *Maynard* a
Pound of Bohea Tea and 3 Onz. of
Sinage Red, as to a leading [line]
Dugdale has promifed to make one
ready to fend by next opportunity
that offers, and at the fame time
will fend Red beet feed. I don't
hear as yet when the Govr Defigns
to fet out for his Journey to *Burlington*. My not finding *Mofs* in
his fhop therefore can fay nothing
as to the Ax.

I am &c.

I BOBIN.

To Mr. *Clarke*.

Edward Hyde to Isaac Bobin.

Sir

I MUST beg ye favor you will send young Mr. *Pamerton* for my Old hatt wch the Bearer hereof will Bring; I aſk pardon for putting you to this Trouble but am Certain Mr. *Bobin* will forgive his

Moſt humble Servt

EDW^D HYDE.

Phœnix Tueſday 9 aClock.

Isaac Bobin to George Clarke.

NEW YORK, SECRY's OFFICE,

February y^e 10th 172$^{8}_{9}$.

Hon^d S^r

H IS Exc^y acquainted me this Day that he deſigns to ſet out from hence for *Burlington* the middle of next week, and thought proper I fhould acquaint you of the fame

I have paid Ten pounds to *Blake's* order according to promife, as like- wife four pounds to *Bernardus Smith* for the ufe of *James Martin*, I have nothing more to add but that I am

Sr

Your moft &c.

To *Geo. Clarke* Efq.

Ifaac Bobin to George Clarke.

NEW YORK, SECRETARY'S OFFICE,
March the 1ft 172⁸⁄₉.

Hond Sir

I RECEIVED yefterday your Let- ter of the 25th of February laft. I have been with Mr. *Phillipfe* for a Copy of Brigadr *Hunter's* Inftruc- tions relating to Patent Officers who

has promifed me a copy of the fame
to morrow, wch I will be Carefull
in forwarding by the firft Opportunity that offers with the other Copys
you mention. Capt *Hopkins* Lottery was Drawn at the City Hall
on Friday laft therefore can fay
nothing as to the Ticketts.

This Morning about the Hour of
One Coll *Heathcote* dyed fuddenly
(as is fayd) of an apopleɩick fit.
As theres no News worthy notice
in Town I have nothing more to
add but that I am &c^a

I Bobin.

To *George Clarke* Efq^r

Iſaac Bobin to Govʳ Burnet.

SECRETARY'S OFFICE, NEW YORK,
March yᵉ 6ᵗʰ 172⁰/₁.

May it pleaſe yoʳ Excellency

THE incloſed on Thurſday laſt was Delivered me by a Boat Man from *Eſoapas* for forwarding to your Excellency. Late laſt Tueſday Night occur'd the Death of Coll. *Heathcote* which was a ſudden ſurprize to the Generality here, I uſe Brevity herein thinking your Excellency ℔ this Poſt will receive it inlarged by Mr. *Hariſon*. I have imployed the opportunity which your Exᶜʸ's abſenſe has afforded in following yoʳ Exᶜʸ's directions relating to the Office, humbly conceiving Sir that at your Return heither you will find it in ſuch Regularity as to receive yoʳ Excellency's approba-

I

tion, for I am ftudious of making
myfelf worthy thereof, being with
the greateft regard,
> S^r

> Your Excellencys
>> Moft humble and
>>> Moft Obed^t Servant
>>>> Is BOBIN.

Ifaac Bobin to George Clarke.

NEW YORK, SECRETARY'S OFFICE,
March y^e 6^{tb} 172$\frac{8}{9}$.

Hon^d Sir

THIS morning yours of yefterday came to hand, I have been
carfull in obferving your directions
relating to the feveral Letters you
fent inclofed, Mr. *Sharpas* has un-
dertaken the forwarding them to
his friend at *Bofton* and at the fame
time will mention to him the taking

the Mafters Receipt, or at leaft to
fend word by what veffell they goe;
he does not doubt of his Correfpond-
ent's care therein and of fending
them from thence to *England* in
the firft Veffell.

S^r I have imployed the opportunity his Excellency's abfence has
afforded me in following yor Orders
concerning the Office, conceiving
that at his Return heither it will
be in fuch Regularity as to Receive
His Excellencys approbation, for I
am ftudious of doing that wch I think

Ifaac Bobin to George Clarke.

NEW YORK, SECRETARY'S OFFICE,
March ye 11th 1720.

Hon^d Sir

INCLOSED is a Copy of Lord
Godolphins Letter to Lord *Corn-
bury* to Reftore Mr. *Byerly* as like-

wife a Copy of his Ex^{cys} Speech to
the Affembly of the *Jerfeys.*

I have paid according to yor order
of the 28th of Febry laft Six pounds
fourteen Shillings to *Jeremiah Smith,*
and in purfuance of y^t of ye 10th
Currant in favour of *John Gilliard*
have bought him a piece of Garlix
at four pounds fifteen fhillings with
wch he feems well contented.

S^r I have ftrech'd a point to
anfwer demands, and as bufinefs of
the Office is not at Prefent fo brifk
as I could wifh therefore defire
you'll give me time to Recruit,
being at a low Ebb,—hope the
fame will be taken into Confideration for I really am with all due
Regard

S^r &c.
I. BOBIN.

S^r

Your Deeds are Recorded.
there's much talk in Town of

his Ex^{cy} and Mrs. *Mary Vanhorn*
the Eldeſt Daughter of *Abraham
Vanhorne.*

Iſaac Bobin to George Clarke.

NEW YORK, *March y^e* 14th 172⅞.

Hon^d Sir

I EMBRACE the opportunity of
Mr. *Mount's* going to the *Plains*
to pay you Mad^m *Clarke* and Mad^m
Hyde my humble regards and to let
you know I received yours of Yeſterday ℥ Mr. *Nicholls.* I will pay
him as ſoon as poſſible your Note
Drawn in his favour I ſhall not be
wanting in my Endeavours to find
out a Sober man to teach your
children & ſo ſoon as I ſucceed
therein will inform you thereof.

Mr. *Wileman* has promiſed without further delay to deliver me to

morrow morning ye Papers belonging to the Office, I have been very
urgent and preffing for the fame, &
fhew'd him that part of yor Letter
relating thereto. I omitted mentioning to you in my laft that I
could not find any mittens in Town
to fuit Mifs *Molly*. I have taken
for you two Ticketts in *Lake's*
Lottery the numbers are 35 & 36.
I ardently wifh fuccefs may attend
them and every thing elfe which
concerns you being with fincerity,
Sir &c.
I. Bobin.

Geo. Clarke Efq.

Iſaac Bobin to George Clarke.

N. Y., *March* yᶜ 21ſt 172¾.

Honᵈ Sir

ACCORDING to yoʳ Requeſt I now ſend by *Blake* four quire of Fine writing Paper; as to Bohea Tea I have given it to good Mr. *Sharpas* who very readyly accepted of the care thereof, and has likewiſe for you a Letter delivered me by *Braſier* from *Eſoapas* for forwarding as directed,—Mr. *Sharpas* deſigns (God willing) to ſet out for the *Plains* to morrow morning about the hour of Nine.

Sʳ Nothing has occurred worthy notice ſince my laſt therefore ſhall conclude with my hearty wiſhes for the proſperity of your good Family and am &c.   Yours

I BOBIN.

To *Geo Clarke* Eſq.

Iſaac Bobin to George Clarke.

N. Y., Secry's Ofeice,
March yᵉ 25ᵗʰ 1721.

Honᵈ Sir

YOURS of yeſterday came to hand. I very well remember what you therein mention in Relation to the Thirty pounds to be allowed you by Col. *Schuyler* out of his Fees on the Patents of Mr. *Hariſon, Phillipſe* &cᵃ I dont know of any Money he has received on yᵗ ſcore. Mr. *Wileman* tells me there's ſome money in his Hands on that Accᵗ and hopes to Compleat the Remainder in a few Days which as ſoon as done will ſettle that affair. I think myſelf on the ſafe ſide as to yoʳ thirty pounds and ſhould be heartyly ſorry ſhou'd prove otherwiſe through my negleƈt.

As to the Patent of *Jeremiah Schuyler* and Comp^a I will fend you an acc^t of the State thereof in my next and am with Refpect

Yours &c.

I. BOBIN.

To *Geo. Clarke* Efq^r

Ifaac Bobin to George Clarke.

S. O. NEW YORK, *Ap^l* 1, 1721.

Hon^d Sir

I HAVE Received yours of Yefterday ℔ *James Jordain.* Inclofed is the fume of two pounds; they are the fmalleft Bills I could get. I have paid Mr. *Nicholls* five pounds in part of yor Note Drawn in his favour.

I can't fay any thing as yet in Relation to the Patent of *Jeremiah Schuyler* and Comp^a Mr. *Phillipfe*

K

being out of Town, The Affembly
of this Province is further adjournd
to the Nineth of May next.

I am yours &c.

I. Bobin.

To *Geo. Clarke* Efq.

Ifaac Bobin to George Clarke.

NEW YORK, SECRETARY'S OFFICE,

Apl 22d 1721.

Hond Sir

I HAVE fent by *Riche* 4 Barls of
Beef at £1. 16ƒ each (Mr. *De-
lancey* pd the fame price it being the
beft in Town) as likewife 12 ℔ of
Chocolate £1 : 2s Hand Brufh 1ƒ
Sweeping Brufh 10ƒ, ½ a Barl of
Peas 18ƒ, with the Bar'l; 12 Inch
White Pine Boards 10ƒ 3℔ of
Whale bone 16ƒ If any of the be-
fore mentioned particulars Shou'd

not prove to content they'll be taken again upon quick Return. If you approve of the Peas I will fend another half Bar¹ by *Riche* Next opportunity. I have not bought any Ozinbrigs by reafon they afk 19*d* ℔ Ell and for that which is Courfe, the greatnefs of the Price I afcribe to the Scarcity of it for want of Veffells from *Europe*. The Bricks and Limeftone *Riche* Referrs till the next Trip. *Riche* has likewife two Roots of Coronation Pinks given by Mr. *Bayeux;* I fend now by *Anne Sheaf* your Servant, 4. ou of Nutmegs, one D° of Mace and two D° of Cloves.

Sᵗ Since you left the town We have not had Weather to Dry Snuff nor met with the good fuccefs of geting Limes &c. but hope to fucceed in both before another Opportunity offers.

(76)

Sr Bufinefs of the Office is very
Dull and nothing occur'd worthy
notice Since yor Departure hence.
therefore Conclude as I really am
&c.

> Yours &c.
>> I. Bobin.

Geo. Clarke Efq.

Ifaac Bobin to George Clarke.

NEW YORK, SECRETARY'S OFFICE,
April ye 26th 1721.

Hon^d Sir

I HAVE received yours of the
24th Inft. relating to *Ned Grif-
fith*; the Moneys paid for nurfing
his Child is four pounds ten fhillings,
being for five Months from the 24th
of November laft to ye 24th Inft. by
which it appears he is ov^r paid
Seven fhillings and nine pence.

S^r I hope you have received my Letter of the 22^d Inſt. in which I have given an Acc^t of the ſeveral things ſent ℔ *Riche* whereby you'll perceive he has been Remiſs in the not Delivering of the Boards, Whale Bone and Coronation Pink Roots. What elſe is wanting he referred ye taking till next Trip, I am with all due Regard   S^r

Yours &c.

Is Bobin.

George Clarke Eſq^r.

Iſaac Bobin to George Clarke.

New York, Secry's Office,

May ye 13th 1721.

Hon^d Sir

I RECEIVED yeſterday by *Tom Hill* yours of the 11th Inſt. and am glad the fruit met with your

kind acceptance as often as I get
fome will fend. I am much obliged
to Mifs *Molly* for her good wifh and
dont doubt but her pretty Genius
will foon make her miftrefs of her
Pen.

S'r I fend inclofed Mr. *Nicholls*
Note as likewife your Quarterly
Warr'ᵗ and three pounds in fmall
Bills, I will Endeavour to compleat
what you wrote me in Relation to
the Patentees; heartily wifh that
affair Laye not fo long Dormant — I
Send now by *Tom Hill* two Bufhells
of Salt at 2ſ ℔ Bufh and two Bafs,
they begin to grow fcarce.

Mrs. *Ludlow* tells me the Child-
rens Cloaths will be ready to Try
next Monday come Seven night.

S'r The Gov'ʳ arrived here from
Amboy Monday laft in y'ᵉ afternoon
and return'd there y'ᵉ Wednefday
morning following; his making fo

fhort a ftay I did not think proper
to trouble you; he is expected back
to morrow, I will fend ℞ next opportunity a Copy of the Speaches
and Addreffes during the fitting of
the Affembly of yᵉ Jerfeys at *Burlington*; the Affembly here is ad-
journed till Tuefday next. There
is no News in Town therefore
concludes as I really am
&c.

I. BOBIN.

George Clarke Efqʳ.

Ifaac Bobin to George Clarke.

NEW YORK, SECRETARY'S OFFICE,

May yᵉ 17ᵗʰ 1721.

Honᵈ Sir,

I HAVE paid *Blake* yoʳ notes of
yᵉ 16ᵗʰ of March laft and the 15ᵗʰ
Inft. drawn in his favour.

Mr. *Wileman* paid me £15 on acc^t of the Patent of *Francis Harrifon* & Comp^a and the patents of *Philip Schuyler* & Comp^a and promifed me (as he has done often) to finifh wth the Patentees this week.

S^r I fend you inclofed a Copy of Speeches & addrefs during the fiting of the Affembly at *Burlington* &c^a

'Tis fayd great preparations are making for the match fo much talked of. Nothing of Novelty has occurd fince my laft therefore conclude as I really am with Sincerity

S^r

Yours &c.

Is Bobin.

Geo. Clarke Efq^r

Isaac Bobin to George Clarke.

NEW YORK, SECRY'S OFFICE,
June ye 5th 1721.

Hon^d Sir

AFTER a Paſſage of Eight weeks from *London* arrived here this Day the Ship *Beaver* wch brings no other news (as I can Learn) than the Death of the Duke of *Buckingham*, Earl *Stanhope*, Earl of *Gallway* and Mr. Secretary *Craggs*, as likewiſe the unhappy Circumſtances the People of *England* groan under by the Conduct of the South Sea Comp^{ay}

His Ex^{cy} delivered to me the Incloſed for forwarding and not knowing the conſequence of the ſame thought it my duty to Diſpatch the Bearer with the ſame hoping my readyneſs will be lookt on no other than that I am with all due Regard.

L

Isaac Bobin to George Clarke.

NEW YORK, SECRETARY'S OFFICE,

June y 6*th* 1721.

Hon^d Sir.

ACCORDING to order, I have paid *Walter Jones* thirty Shillings and nine pence, And now send by him a pound of Bohea Tea twelve pound of starch and a Paper of Ink Powder.

I am sorry for your misfortune in breaking the Wheele of your Chase; But hope Mad^m *Clark* nor yourself have met with no hurt thereby, I will observe what you wrote me in Relation to Chariot Wheels, Lead &c^a.

Mad^m *Hyde* sent me the inclosed for forwarding. Mr. *Hyde* seems under Concern for his past Conduct which he has promised to Regulate

for the future. I ardently wifh he may hold his Refolution. And am
&c.

I. BOBIN.

P. S. *Wm Ellifon*, Mas of the Sloop *W^m* will Sail for *London* about the middle of Next Week.

Ifaac Bobin to George Clarke.

NEW YORK, SECRETARY'S OFFICE,

June ye 15th 1721.

Hon^d Sir

HIS Excellency has Commanded me to acquaint you that he defires you'll pleafe to favour him with your prefence here this Week.

Before yours of the 16th Inftant came to hand, I fent by *Riche* Sixty Bufhells of Lime at 1 *f* ℔ Bufhell, As to Lathing Nails and Cedar Bolts

I shall send them by the first opportunity and will be mindfull of the
Chariot Wheels.

Mr. *DeLancy* is not certain when
the *Beaver* will fail, but Believes
the Beginning of next week. Capt
Smith has promised to let me know
y^c certainty thereof in a day or two.

Laft Council Day Capt. *Walter*,
Coll *Beekman*, Mr. *Van Dam*, Mr.
Barberie and Mr. *Phillipfe* or any
three of them were appointed a
Committee of the Affembly to Examin the late Treafurer's Accounts
and accordingly met at Coll *Depeyfter's* Houfe on Saturday laft for that
purpofe.

I. Bobin.

Mr *Hyde* is very much reformed.
To *George Clarke* Efq^r

Iſaac Bobin to George Clarke.

NEW YORK, SECRY'S OFFICE,

July yᵉ 5ᵗʰ 1721.

Honᵈ Sir

THE members of the Council in Town being but few and Mr. *Phillipſe* declining to act upon Mr. *Baker's* News of his Removal from yᵉ Council (which his Exᶜʸ believes to be true tho' he has had no advice of the ſame.) his Excellency has therefore ordered me to acquaint you that he deſires your preſence in Town here to Act and aſſiſt in Council.

The Particulars ſent by *Riche* are as follows. The Medicines for the Doctor; the Acct ſent by Mr. *Hyde;* Teſtament and Pſalter 4ſ6; a Barrel of Brown Sugar, a Barrel of Rum; a Barrˡ of Molaſſes £3 4ſ 6d; 1 pᵈ of Gun Powder 2ſ 6d; 8 Dᵒ of Shot 3ſ; 3. pᵈ of Lathing Nails 3ſ 3d; 64. pᵈ of Candles £2;—a Loaf of Sugar quantity 27. pᵈ at 18d ℔ pᵈ; 12 yds½ of Garlix 2ſ 9d.

Coll. *Rutſen* puts one off from Day to Day Courtier like, but ſays that if he fail this week he ſhall think himſelf very unworthy of any favours from you for the future. I have not received from the Treaſurer your Quarterly warrᵗ ending June laſt. I have nothing more to add but that I am.

Honᵈ Sir &c.

I. Bobin.

Ifaac Bobin to George Clarke.

NEW YORK, SECRETARY'S OFFICE,
Augt ye 1ft 1721.

Hon^d Sir —

I HAVE finifhed with Mr. *Hyde* and got every thing neceffary for his voyage put on Board, Capt *Downing* propofes to fail to Day, the Owners would not give Credit for Mr. *Hyde's* Paffage Money, therefore have been obliged to draw ten pounds from the Gov^{rs} fees, The amount of his Accounts is 1 58*l* 1*s* 0¾ New York money, wch I have re- duced to Sterl^g and taken his Receipt for the fame.

There is only gone by *Riche* laft Trip Six Cedar Bolts The Lime he Refufed to take on Board, it muft therefore go by next Trip with what elfe is wanting; he tells me

he will be in Town the latter end of
this week, The ten pounds Drawn
in his favor being not yet paid makes
him very furly wch I cant help.   I
was yefterday at the Treafurer's who
fays he has none

I am yours
I Bobin.

Ifaac Bobin to George Clarke.

NEW YORK, SECRETARY'S OFFICE,
Auguft ye 21ſt 1721.

Hon^d Sir.

H IS Ex^cy gave me this morning
the Enclofed for forwarding;
he defigns to Imbark for *Albany* on
Thurfday next.

Mr. *Mount* is fo kind to favour
me with his Care of this & Mad^m
Clarke's Snuff Box, and to take the
Trouble of a Canifter of Bohea
Tea, The bearer of your Letter of

the 19th not coming near me but delivered the Letter to a Soldier.

S^r I have according to order paid *David Cathair* four pounds. The Chaife Wheels are Ready to fend by *Riche;* old *Read* dyed on Friday laft. Capt *Lancelot* maf^r of y^e *John* Gally bound to *London* from *Jamaica* was neceffitated to come here, the Veffell proving very Leaky will fail for *London* in about Eight Days, and Capt *Ouvery* about the middle of next month.

Ifaac Bobin to George Clarke.

NEW YORK, SECRETARY'S OFFICE,
September ye 12th 1721.

Hon^d Sir.

WITH fome Struggle I have conquered that troublefome Companion the feaver and Ague,

M

by checking it in time; I am told
that at *Amboy* there is not one Houfe
free from that difeafe, fome the
whole family Down, and is almoft
as brieff here; I heartyly wifh your
good family may efcape it.

S^r   Inclofed is an Account of the
feveral particulars fent now ℞ *Riche*
by your order for the ufe of Doctor
Magrath; there gos likewife a loaf
of fine Sugar (w^{ch} *Cæfar* left behind
him when you were laft in Town)
at 2*f* 3*d* p^r   The Chaife Wheels
likewife go this trip.

I have paid Mrs. *Tarr* fifty fhillings on acc^t of the Note Drawn in
her Hufband's favour; had made
her eafy as to the remainder by
promife where She ow'd Money to
pay it in a little time wch has anfwer'd her End.

The Genl Complaint here is a
Confumption of Trade & your

Office is not without a taſte of the
unhappy effect of a Languiſhing
Commerce, buſineſs being ſo dull
that I have not for this Six Days
or more cleared a veſſel or taken
any money in yᵉ Office. The Treaſurer ſays he has none in his hands
and does not know when he ſhall,
wᶜʰ makes ſome Officers who have
quarterly Warrᵗˢ look with Droop-
ing aſpects fearing they will be
obliged to paſs the Winter upon the
faith and Credit of an Honᵇˡᵉ Sup-
port without Money. The Govʳ is
expected here the Begginning of
next week.

Isaac Bobin to George Clarke.

NEW YORK, SECRETARY'S OFFICE,

September ye 14th 1721.

Hon^d Sir

I HAVE received yours of the 12th Inft. by *Peter Smith* and according to order fend by *Tunis Snediker* the Keg filled with Lime Juice I will be mindfull of Peach Stones.

Tuefday laft I fent by *Riche* what was wanting for Doctor *Magrath,* and a loaf of fine Sugar w^{ch} *Cæfar* left behind him.

The Govr unexpected arrived here this morning about the Hour of Six. I dont hear as yet what progrefs he has had with the Indians.

S^r I return you thanks for the Concern you Exprefs for my Welfare & my late Indifpofition. I thank God I am recovered and am now in a perfect ftate of health. I hope your goodfelf and family are the like and that they may be bleft with the Continuance of yᵉ fame is the fervent wifh of

Sʳ

Ifaac Bobin to George Clarke.

NEW YORK, SECRETARY'S OFFICE,
Sept. yᵉ 27ᵗʰ 1721.

Honᵈ Sir.

THERE goes now ℔ *Riche* a pound of Bohea Tea; 6 yds of brown Ozinbriggs; four ½ of blew Dᵒ

Sʳ I have been with yᵉ Pump maker named *Richᵈ Talbot*, who fends you the inclofed and fays he Can't pretend to undertake yᵉ making a Pump for lefs than 2ʃ ℔

Foot, for it is the ufual and Cuf-
tomary price and y^t he expects 8f
🝓 Diem during the time that he
fhall be at the *Plains* affixing &
feting the fame, And his Charges
and Expences both going and returning, wch I told I thought was fome
what out of ye way, therefore told
him I could do nothing further
before I had acquainted you there-
with and know your pleafure, which
as foon as it came to hand would
let him know — he anfwered if you
agreed to what he propofed he would
fall upon the work forthwith and
give it all immediate difpatch. Mr.
Sharpas tells me he is a Mafter of
his bufinefs.

S^r I acquainted his Excellency
that you prefented to him your Duty
and y^t your being much out of order
with a Cold in y^r head and a fore
throat hindred your waiting on him;

he made me no anſwer ; I repeated
the ſame word to him a ſecond
time, he ſtill was ſilent; then I
withdrew.

Sʳ The Office is very bare of
money and will not anſwer for what
is drawn for Sundrys and as I have
been hitherto obliged when I had
not caſh in hands to take things on
yoʳ Credit, and buſineſs ſince not
having been briſk enough to anſwer
other Demands and Diſcharge that,
therefore People are ſhye in Delivering there goods without ready
money, wᶜʰ I know not how [to get.]

Ifaac Bobin to George Clarke.

New York, Secrys Office,
Octobr 18th 1721.

Hon^d Sir

I HAVE received your Letter of ye 17th Inft. by yor Negro & will leave no ftone unturned to get in what money I can, but am at prefent very bare, being obliged now to pay ready money for what things I take up for your ufe ; when a Sum comes to hand I fhall inform you thereof with great pleafure. I have writ to Coll *Rutfen* & wait dayly for his anfwer. Mr. *Wileman* yefterday acquainted me that he had rec'd a Letter from Mr. *Collins* of *Albany*, date ye 4 Inf^t in which he prefents you his humble duty and defires to be excufed for his long filence and y^t he will make fpeedy payment of your Fees, and in order thereto Mr. *Bickly* has prepared a quantity of Flower and Peas to fend to *York* to be fold fo that Money may be dayly hoped for. Neverthelefs I will obferve your Directions to Mr. *Bickley*.

I fend now by *Will* a Loaf of fingle refin'd Sugar q^t 7 p^d at 1 f, 6d ⅌ p^d; 13 yds of Duffles at 6f 3d; four yds of Swanfkin at 4f; 3 Indian Brooms 1f: 2 Bibles, 18f;—they are beft I could get & am forry the Print is not better; as to *Venice* talk [? chalk] there is none in Town; Doctor *Nicholls* had fome a few days ago but it is all fold to ye Ladys.

I fend by *Will* four pounds in fmall Bills &c.

I am

S^r

Yours &c^a

I Bobin.

N

Ifaac Bobin to George Clarke.

NEW YORK, SECRETARY'S OFFICE,
October yᵉ 26ᵗʰ 1721.

Honᵈ Sir

WILL carrys with him feven yards of yallow Taffita and as much of Blew at 10ſ. & 6d ℔ yard,— & ½ oz of Blew Sowing filk; if not likt will be taken again; Mrs. *Ludlow* tells me the yallow fuits very well, and the Blew is the neareft the Patern I could get & fays fhe can't go to the *Plains* before the Beginning of next week, her hands being full of work. I have had the happinefs of feeing Mifs *Katty* yefterday Evening. Mr. *Sharpas* and Mʳˢ *Betty Sharpas* conceiving Mifs wou'd want a Night Gown I have therefore bought as much Calico as will make a double Gown

and had Mrs. *Betty's* advice therein,
what elfe Mifs may want I will take
care to furnifh. Mrs. *Ludlow* will
make it forthwith. Mifs *Katty*
went with Mrs. *Braffier* in Mr.
Bickeley's   laft night. Mr.
Fauconnier is not in Town and can't
Larn when he is Expected.

I will obferve what you write in
relation to *Rhode Ifland* Cheefes as
I fhall do in every thing elfe.

I have writ to Mr. *Collins* as or-
dered and have forwarded a Second
Letter to Coll *Rutfen* very prefling.
I expect dayly to hear from them.

I am much obliged to Mifs *Molly*
for her kind Remembrance of me,
and to affure when I go to the
Sweat Garden have her in my
thoughts; have now fent her fome.

There is no news. Mr. *Haring-*
ton promifed to give me fome Limes,
but has not been fo good as his

word tho' often calling has not been
wanting.

I am with Refpect

S^r

&c.

Is Bobin.

To Mr *Clarke*.

Ifaac Bobin to George Clarke.

New York, Secry's Office,

Novr ye 24th 1721.

Hon^d Sir

I RECEIVED yr Letter of Yefterday about Seven in the Evening ♄ *Will* and am forry to hear
Blake has proved fuch a Villain, I
have not feen him fince I paid him
your note Drawn in his favour w^{ch}
was Thurfday laft nor dont hear
now y^t he is in Town, therefore
have forwarded with Inftructions a

Writt to the Sheriff of *Richmond*
County & will be diligent in making
further inquiry after him. As to
the Sashes they were not made at
Smiths but at one *Peacocks* in the
Broadway who not being at home
therefore have rec'd no jnformation
thereof, but shall obferve your directions relating thereto—I dont
hear that he has left any thing at
Riches—

Mr. *Phillips* and Mr. *Sharpas*
prefent you their humble fervice
and fay they'll referr the drawing
Lotts till you come to Town.

I fend by *Will* five yd^s of plain
fuftain at 3*ʃ*, 3*d* but am afraid its
too Corfe there is none figured in
Town; if not likt will be taken
upon Return I fend likewife 2 yds
of Blew Duffles at 6*ʃ* ℔ yd.

I will Inquire after another
Joyner.

Iſaac Bobin to George Clarke.

NEW YORK, S. OFFICE,
Novr yᵉ 26 1721.

Hon Sir

I REC'D yeſterday your Letters of yᵉ 8ᵗʰ and 15ᵗʰ Inſᵗ   The Sevˡ Part. mention'd in that of the 8ᵗʰ go now by *Riche* Vizᵗ a Barrˡ of Sugar from Mʳ *Schuyler*; Six pʳ of gloves for Madᵐ *Clarke* at 3ſ a pʳ 6 Sheets of Miniken pins 8ſ.; 12 of largeſt 16ſ—; 12 of the Middling, 11ſ.; 2 Small Cords & large Bedd Cord — 11ſ; thirty two Gallons of Moloſſes *Jamaica* the beſt in Town 2ſ. ₱ Gallon; Six qʳ of Letter Paper & 6 of Copying Paper; a Maſons Trowell, 3ſ.; Six Packs of Cards 7ſ 6d; Three Ivory Combs 5ſ 6d; 1 horn Comb 3d If any of the prices of the before mention'd particulars bought by me, fhou'd be thought unreafonable or not likt by Mad^m *Clarke* they will be taken again upon Return — I have been Carefull y^t the Sugar and Moloffes can are well hoop'd.

S^r I return you my hearty thanks for the trouble you have taken to fend me my Fathers Letter, as alfo of my kinfman and am under fome Concern to pceive my friends at home uneafy for want of hearing from me ; however Letters have mifcarryed I can't tell, but as I have always had a value and efteem for my Parents therefore have never been wanting when opportunity of- fered to let them know of my Welfare.

S^r I have paid *Blake* yor Note Drawn in his favour for five pounds *Sconlock* not having Money to advance, and finding him under

neceffity to buy hinges Nails &c^a
for the ufe of your houfe; which
he told me was very much expofed
to Weather, mov'd me to ftretch a
point.

I will fend what elfe is wanting
⅌ *Riche* next Trip which he tells
me will be the Latter End of next
week — Yo^r Warrants upon Mr.
Byerly are figned.

Coden has promifed to bring fome
good R. *Ifland* Cheefe for your
Winter Store. I have paid Mr.
Selby your note of One pound ten
fhillings drawn in his favour.

Capt *Smith* of y^e *Beaver* Informs
that he fhall fail the Latter End of
next Week hoping to Eat to his
Xmas dinner in *London*

I can get no Money from The
Treafurer, nor have not been fo
happy as to receive a Line from Coll
Rutfen tho' I have often writ. I

have received from Mr. *Collins* yo[r]
fees out of w[ch] I have paid *Riche*.

His Ex[cy] is Expected from *Amboy*
Sunday next. Miſs *Katty* is very well.

The Surveyor Gen[l] has not yet
made any Return of y[e] Surveys of
the Land laid out for D[r] *Humes* &
al. As to *Anthony* I refer to his
Letter Incloſed.

Blake will Inform you concerning
Cedar Bolts.

I begg you'll excuſe the broken
Engliſh of my Father's Letter Ill
ſee that ſome Snuff be made &c.

Iſaac Bobin to George Clarke.

New York, S. Office,
February y[e] 21[ſt] 172½.

Hon[d] Sir

THERE goes now by *Riche* The
Barrel of Sugar, Box of Candles, Six Indian Brooms, & Eight

O

pound of Chalck. The Punch &
marking Iron are not finifhed.

    Sr Since my laft to you I have
received a Letter from Coll *Rutfen*
wherein he jnforms me that he has
found two Mares one large about 6
or 7 years old and the other three
next Spring the price of wch are fix
pound each that he has likewife got
one large Drawing Horfe a Black
Ball above 15 hands high 5 years
old at £15. That he will ufe his
utmoft Endeavour to get another to
match him, but in the mean time
defires my anfwer upon the fame.
I therefore crave you'll be pleafed
to let me know whether you think
thofe prices reafonable or not, that
I may thereby be the better enabled
to make an anfwer thereto, There
will be no opportunity of fending
before the latter End of next week.

Isaac Bobin to George Clarke.

SECRETARY'S OFFICE, N. YORK,
March ye 7th 172⅚.

Hon^d Sir

I HAVE received yor Letter of the 5th Inftant by *Will* inclofed in the Warrants you write for & as concerning Deeds all thofe that were in my care I fend now in the Trunk for that purpofe together with thofe found in yor Scrutoire at Mr. *Schuyler's* as likewife Mr. *Byerly's* Mortgages. The Deeds Recorded are Seperate from the others and are diftinguifhed by a Labell—I have Inquired of Mr. *Sharpas* and Mr. *Wileman* whether they had any Deeds belonging to you who told me they [had] not any. I will Endeavour to get Cedar Bolts to fend by *Riche* next Conveyance, and Copy the Bills of the Lawyers to go at the fame time

I have given Mrs. *Ludlow* 5 yds of plain White Calicote at 5ſ ⅌ yard; 2 yds of plain Muſlin at 9ſ; a Doz. of Knives & Forks at 8ſ; Thread 9ſ; four Combs & Bruſh 6ſ & 9d; Baſs 2ſ. Dear Sʳ I hope you'll excuſe my keeping *Will* Yeſterday being Called to my Relation on *Long Iſland* who had a pain on yᶜ ſide and moreover the Deeds recorded took me ſome time to Examine I am &c.

I. BOBIN.

P. S.
  Sir.
  I ſend by *Will* in ſmall money two pounds three Shillings being all I had to ſpare having over drawn the Governours fees as believe your're ſenſible.

I have paid yor two Notes of y^e
22^d of Febry laſt in favour of *Ma-
rias Marſh* & *Heſter Grice.*

Iſaac Bobin to George Clarke.

Secretary's Office, New York,
January ye 10th 172⅞.

Hon^d Sir.

I HAVE been with Mr. *Lane* concerning the Negro Wench, who
tells me he has her now in his
Houſe, and is willing to let you
have her upon Tryal not doubting
but you'll find her a good ſlave ; I
will take care that ſhe be ſent by
Riche.

Sr The Report of the Committee
to whom was referred your account
of Incidents of your Office has been
read in Council, but upon ſome
Gentlemen oppoſing the confirma-

tion thereof it was recommitted, and
fo remains and for no other reafon
than that they fay you ought not to
be allowed for Blank Let Paffes and
Lycences, which have been allowed
hitherto, At the fame time your
Warrant for payment of your years
falary out of the Quit-rents Ending
the 13th of December laft, was
likewife read and laid before his
Excellency for Signing, but was fet
afide it being objected by fome at
that Board, that if your Warrant
paffed with thefe Words viz.t [to
be paid preferrable to all other
Eftablifhments] (which words are
grounded upon a Minute of Council) they could never expect to
receive their Salarys for that yours
would always be accordingly paid
the firft, and that thereby they
fhou'd be difcouraged in the profe-
cution of their Offices, thereupon

moved that a minute might be
made that no more was meant or
intended by the word [preferrable]
than that Warrants for payment of
the faid Salary be always preferrably
paid to Warrants upon the faid
Fund and the fame date and be
accordingly the firft number of fuch
Warrants, which was agreed to by a
Majority of the Board, and Ordered
that the Warrant be drawn Con-
formable.

Your being acquainted of thefe
matters as well as having a view of
what I am going further to obferve
will fhew how finifterly fome people
are inclin'd and in order thereto
I fend you inclofed the Copy of
Minutes of the Committee appointed to Examin the Abftract of
Patents, the firft Paragraph of the
fecond Minute I think with fub-
miffion is jnduftrioufly Pen'd with

an jntent to reproach the Office, for
the Minute there mentioned to be
wanting is not of any confequence
or of any greater moment than a
loofe half fheet of Paper with fome
Remarks or Obfervations on Patents
and other Records and which was
miflay'd by themfelves, but the fame
being fince found that part of the
Minute is obliterated and they now
feem to take little notice of the
reft, Notwithftanding I further obferved that towards the conclufion
of the fourth Paragraph of the faid
Minutes they took Notice that a
great many of the Minutes of Council are wanting and not mentioning
what Minutes.   I lookt upon thofe
words to be General and fearfull
they were couch'd with fome defign,
I therefore advifed with Mr. *Bickley*
to know whether thofe words if
Reported in that manner might hurt

you in your Office, who made me
eafy in that particular by telling me
that the Beginning of the faid Paragraph fully explain'd that they are
old Records, that are wanting, for
which you could not be anfwerable
being that feveral were carried to
Bofton by Sr *Edmund Androfs*.

As I have ever lookt upon thofe
Gentlemen with a Watchfull Eye,
fo fhall at all times be wakefull in
obferving every thing that may be
for ye fafety of your jntereft being
with great truth and refpect

S^r

&c

I hope you've heard of your
Trunk

P

Isaac Bobin to George Clarke.

Secry's Office, New York,
Jany ye 14th 1722.

Hon^d Sir

THE inclofed Letter I purpofd to fend by Capt *Congreve* who promif'd to call for the fame but forgot.

I have received yours of the 12th jnftant and will be punctual in paying Mr. *Kennedy's* mother the fum therein mentioned.

I fend by *Will* 10 p^d of Hops at 1*f* 3*d* 12 p^r of Kid Gloves at 4*f* 6*d* 2 packs of Cards 3*f*, 12 yd^s Woorfted Feriting 2*f* 3*d*; 2 Bed Cords 9*f*; & 6 p^d of Floor Nails 5*f*. As to the Negro Wench I beg leave to referr to the inclofed Letter and am

Yours &c.

I am glad to hear *Riche* remembers the Trunk —

I have been jnformed by one that had a mind to purchaſe the ſaid Wench about a twelve Month ago that he offered the ſame Sum her Maſter does now aſk but that he then inſiſted upon fifty pounds.

I have paid your note in favour of *Jnᵒ Henderſon*

The Governour goes for *Jerſey* on Tueſday or Wedneſday morning next.

Iſaac Bobin to George Clarke.

Secretary's Office, New York,
Janry yᵉ 27ᵗʰ 172⅜.

Honᵈ Sir

I HAVE yours of the 26ᵗʰ; that for Mr. *Walpole* I have taken care to put into the Greyhound News bagg with my own hands.

I fend by *Will* a pound of Bohea Tea at £1. 4ſ. as likewife a pair of blew Coarfe ſtockings at 3ſ. If not likt will be taken again upon return — I went this morning upon the Market to look for freſh Fiſh, but did not fee any. Inclofed is three pounds one ſhill in ſmall Bills.

Captain *Munro* has a young Negro Wench to difpofe off between 16 & 17 years of age born at *Jamaica* in the *Weſt Indies* but brought up here fince three years old, he is not willing to let her go upon Tryall, but will warrant her to be found Limbed and a garl that may be train'd up to any manner of bufi- nefs, the price is forty five pounds which he fays he gave for her three years ago to Mr. *Dunck*, I have Enquired into her Character among thofe of the Neighborhood who jnform me that ſhe is a good ſlave.

The reaſon of parting from her I believe is the want of Money. *Will* can give ſome account of her, having ſeen her.

I will make a Copy of your laſt year's acc^t of Incidents and ſend by next opportunity and am with due regaŕd

Hon^d Sir
&c^a

Iſaac Bobin to George Clarke.

February ye 8th 172⅞.

Hon^d Sir

I RECEIVED Yeſterday Evening yours of the 6th jnſtant by *Will.* Incloſed is three pounds in ſmall Bills.

I have been with Mrs. *Schuyler* and acquainted her with what you deſired. She deſires me to Let you

know that fhe put afide for you a
pair of Gloves and a Scraff which
She now fends by *Will* and prays
you'll pleafe to accept of the fame.
The poor woman feems under a
great concern for the lofs of her
hufband, I have had from her a
half p^s of *Holland* Linewn q^t 26
Ells; a p^s of Cambrick; 2 p^s of
Tape at 1ſ 6 p^r p^s; & 1 Ditto at 2ſ
as likewife a p^s of brown Ozibrigg
q^t 72 Ells at 19d. Upon inquiry I
find it is as good & cheap as thofe
bought at the Merchants all which
now goes by *Will* together with
25 p^d of twelve penny nails at 10d
℔ £; Six long filk Laces at 1ſ 6d
a p^s; Six yd^s of white Corded Dim-
mity at 4ſ ℔ yd; an Ounce of
Camphire 5ſ.; a pint of Spirits of
Wine 6ſ.; 12 p^d of Hard Soap. a
p^s of Garlix chofe by Mrs. *Ludlow*
£3. 10ſ; As to Loaf Sugar there is
none to be got in Town.

S^r I fend you inclofed a Copy of the Addrefs of the Houfe of Commons to his Majefty which is lately come by the way of *Briftoll* in a Brigantine belonging to *Abraham Vanhorn.* She brings little or no news; the Lords in the Tower are not yet brought to Tryal. I am now preparing his Excellencys orders to the Judge of the Pleas in ye feveral Countys relating to the Probate of Wills &c^a His Excellency declines appoing Surrogates in the remote Countys, and as to Apprazers Mr. *Harifon* and Coll *Lurting* have the power of Deputation. I am with all due regard.

Hon^d Sir

Yours &c.

I have difpatched *Will* with all Expedition — It is now between twelve and one.

Iſaac Bobin to George Clarke.

SECRY'S OFFICE, NEW YORK,
March yᵉ 13ᵗʰ 172⅔.

Honᵈ Sir

I HAVE paid yoʳ note of the 12ᵗʰ inſt in favour of Mr. *Temple* to his wife by whom I now ſend a few Oranges which I hope will meet with your and Madᵐ *Clarkes* acceptance I am ſorry Limes are ſo ſcarce that I cant get any.

The Particulars ſent by *Will* when laſt in Town are as follows Vizᵗ Two Groſs of Corks 7ſ; a pˢ of Cherconne Romacks £3; a Tin Funnell 1ſ 3d; 3 pˢ of *Holland* Tape 7ſ; a Loaf of Double refind Sugar qᵗ 3½ at 2ſ. 7½ ; a pᵈ of Bohea Tea £1. 4, & two Packs of Cards 2ſ. 6d—

I have been with *Jones* concerning a wigg, who has promiſed me to make one according to defire againſt April next.

Yeſterday arrived in the Evening *Andrew Biſſet*, Maſter of the *Snow Hamilton*, who left *London* the 7ᵗʰ of December laſt and the 26 following from the *Downs* to *Maderas* Arrived ſome time in January, by whom we have the following advice That Councilor *Leare* was Tryed and Condemned and that ſome time in January was aſſigned for his Execution, but upon his propoſalls of making a full diſcovery was reprieved for two months, and that the Lord Biſhop of *Rocheſter* and the other Lords in the Tower were not brought to Tryal nor it was not known when they would. I have Enquired but do not hear of any Letters for you and am with reſpect

Sʳ

Yours &ᶜ

Q

by *Will* was likewife fent in my Letter £3. 1 —

Ifaac Bobin to George Clarke.

SECRETARY'S OFFICE, NEW YORK,
March yᵉ 19ᵗʰ 172⅜.

Honᵈ Sir

I HAVE received yours of Yefterday by *Will* I fend now by him
Ropes, Leading Lines, half a pound
of Nutmegs and twelve pound of
ftarch. I have fent to moft places in
Town but Cant get Garden Beans,
thofe that have had any have planted
them, I fent likewife to Mr. *Delancey*
who was forry you did not think of
'em fooner he having made ufe of
all he had. There has not been
any fifh upon the Markets this
Day—What elfe is mentioned in
your Letter I will be punctual in
obferving.

S^r Mr. *Harifon* prefents you his Humble Service as likewife to Mad^m *Clarke* and Mad^m *Hyde*. He is much concerned about a Patent that appears in this Office for 3000 acres of Land on the Weft fide of *Hudfons* River to the Southward of *Old Mans* Creek, granted by Coll *Ingoldfby* to *Wm Glincrofs, Alexander Campbell* and *Thomas Harding*. The faid Patent being for Land for which he has a Grant from Brigad^r *Hunter* and as the faid Patent is prior to his he is Apprehenfive that he will fuffer, but what gives him fome hopes of a remedy is that *Glincrofs* and others have never paid any Quit rent for faid Land nor does faid Patent appear upon Record, neither is it figned by yourfelf or Deputy. He defired me to mention it to you believing you would give him your advice in that affair.

P. S.

Sr *Will*, Since I finiſhed my Letter, has got about a q^t of garden
Beans for wch he has been obliged
to pay 9*d.*

Iſaac Bobin to George Clarke.

SECRETARY'S OFFICE, NEW YORK,

Apl ye 3^d 1723.

Hon^d Sir.

THE Chairs go now by *Riche* as
likewiſe two Barrlls of *Long
Iſland* Beef at £1. 18. ⅌ Bar^l, & the
Box with Candles q^t 63 p^d
I have referred ſending Lime
Juice till another opportunity that
which is now in Town being not
only bad but deer. Veſſells are
dayly expeéted from the *Weſt Indies,*
when they are arrived I will look
out for ſome that is good and at the

fame time Endeavour to get fome fruit for Mad^m *Clarke*.

The Governour will meet the Affembly of this Province the 7th of May next according to the adjournment of that Houfe. I have by his Order fent Circular Letters to acquaint the members thereof. His Excellency will go for *Jerfey* the 23^d of this jnftant—The Veffells mentioned in the inclofed Mercury now at *Amboy* bound for *London* will not fail before the Latter End of this Week or beginning of next. The Govr upon Information that a Malignant Diftemper was raging in the Ifland of *Jamaica*, called a Council whereupon an order was made that the Ferry man at the *Narrows* on *Long Ifland* fide and likewife the Ferry men on *Staten Ifland* do on the approach of any Veffell from Sea repair on Board

every Veffell coming in and if any
of them come from *Jamaica* they
are to forbid them to proceed further than the Watering place under
Staten Ifland till further order.

Mr. *Jemmey Morris* is very bad
of a Confumption in fo much that
his life is dayly difpaired off.

Sʳ I omitted to mention that I
likewife now fend by *Riche* a Barˡ
of Moloffes qᵗ 32 Gal. 21*d* ℔ Gal.

Ifaac Bobin to George Clarke.

SECRETARY'S OFFICE, NEW YORK,

April 17, 1723.

Honᵈ Sir

I HAVE received yours of yᵉ 11ᵗʰ
jnft. by *Riche*, I fend now by him
yᵉ following particulars Vizᵗ five
Gallons of Lime Juice at 2*f*. 6. ℔
Gal ; a Barrˡ of Tarr at 7*f*. 6*d*; a

Gallon of Sallade Oyl 12ʃ; Eleven
fathom of White well Rope, Three
Baʃs, Two Groʃs of Corks at 3ʃ 6d.
I have not found any Ox Cart Boxes
Suitable to the Scize you ʃent, but
ʃhall make further Enquiry. As to
Loaf Sugar there is none in Town
nor has there been as yet any Lob-
ʃter upon Market, And in Caʃh two
fifteen Shilling Bills one of Twenty
and one of Six together with Eleven
dollars, which make in the whole
Six pounds two Shillings.

Sʳ Since my Laʃt there has not
arrived but one Veʃʃell from the
Weʃt Indies which was from *Jamaica*, She brought no fruit, all
the fruit upon that Iʃland being
deʃtroyed by the late Storm they
have had there; the News that a
Contagious Diʃtemper was raging
there proves falʃe.

When Veʃʃells arrive and bring

fruit I will not be wanting to get
fome to fend to the *plains*.

I am
&c.
I. BOBIN.

Geo. Clarke Efq^r

Ifaac Bobin to George Clarke.

Apl ye 19th 1723.

S^r

I HAVE received yours of Yef-
terday. I am forry I can not
find any Ox Cart Boxes to the
Demenfions you defire,—*Walther
Thong* tells me he expects fome
Dayly from *Bofton*.

Coll. *Lurting* inform'd me of a
Negro wench to be difpofed off by
one *Chaloner* who is going to Live
with his Family at *Rhode Ifland*,

Whereupon I went to the said *Chaloner* where I saw the Wench he brought wth him about 3 years ago & is about twenty Years of age; speaks pretty good English, Sound Limb, understand every thing belonging to Houshold affairs (as her Master inform'd me). The Lowest price he tells me is forty five pounds ready money and will not let her go upon Tryal. I omitted to mention that ye wench is Six months gone wth Child as her M^r told me.

I am commanded by his Ex^{cy} & Coun^l to send you the jnclosed Minute of which you are to take notice and Govern yourselves accordingly.

R

Iſaac Bobin to Mrs. Hyde.

SECRETARY'S OFFICE, NEW YORK,
June ye 8th 1723.

Madam.

I HAVE received yours of Yeſterday by *Will*, & am ſorry to
hear of Mr. *Clarkes* Indiſpoſition.
I wiſh him his health as likewiſe
all ye family.

Madam

I ſend now by *Will* 8 Lobſters
& 27 Crabbs; a pound of Bohea
Tea £1. 4 as likewiſe fifty ſhillings
in ſmall Bills. I will obſerve what
you write me in relation to Miſs
Molly, and will pay Mr. *Cook* two
Piſtolls according to deſire — I am
concern'd to hear that the thought
of Miſs *Molly Dickens* not being
paid for the Silk Stockings ſhould
give you any uneaſineſs. I hope ſhe

has not been fo unkind as to afk
you or Mr. *Clarke* for it when in
Town, for I paid it her imediately
after ordered, fhe may Remember I
gave her a Piftoll and fhe had not
change to give me; I have her Receipt which will Reconcile that
matter, I give you Mr. *Clarke* and
Mad^m *Clarke* Joy of mafter *Hyde's*
recovery and am with refpect.
Mad^m &c.

Ifaac Bobin to George Clarke.

Secretary's Office, New York,
July 2^d 1723.

Hon^d Sir

I HAVE yours of Yefterday, I
have been with *Jno Chambers*
and received from him 44 Ounces
and a half of Plate   I fend by *Cæfar*
a Teftament and Spelling Book as
likewife fome Lobfters.

We hear from *Albany* that Coll
John Schuyler has been difcovered
to Trade with *Canada*.

I. BOBIN.

George Clarke Efq^r.

Ifaac Bobin to George Clarke.

SECRETARY'S OFFICE, NEW YORK,

July ye 12th 1723.

Hon^d Sir.

I RECEIVED this morning your
Letter of Yefterday, & will obferve what you write now concerning
a Welfh Dairy made, as well what
you mention relating to *Allane
Jarret.* *Lawrence* has never fpoke
to me about any maid.

I will Enquire of *Cook* to day
when Mifs *Mollys* month is expired
and pay him. I fend by *Will* 32
Gallons of Rum at 3*f.* 3*d.*

I have paid *Molly Sheppard* four pounds.

As to Mr. *Byerlys* Mortgage I believe 'tis among the Deeds I ſent you according to the deſire of your Letter of the 5th of March, 172½.

Iſaac Bobin to George Clarke.

SECRETARY'S OFFICE, NEW YORK,
July ye 17th 1723.

Hon^d Sir

I HAVE received yours of the 13th jnſt. what you obſerve therein concerning Mr. *Byerly's* Mortgage is very Juſt, for upon ſecond thought I remembred I had it from you and gave it to Mr. *Wileman* (who now has it) in order for to make oath to the Execution of it, which he has not as yet done, but has promiſed me to do it   out of hand

this week. I will not be wanting
in often calling upon him till it is
compleated and then Record it.

I have fpoke to *Lawrence* who
tells me he has not as yet heard of
a Maid, but will ufe his utmoft
Endeavour to get one,— *Allane Jarratt* is not yet arrived.

I have delivered your Letter to
the Treafurer — I have paid the
Bearer your Note in his favour.

Mr. *Boelen*, the Dutch Lawyer,
who is concern'd for the Perfons
naturaliz'd complain'd to his Excellency that I infifted upon twenty
fhillings for each Perfon named in
the Act whereupon his Ex^{cy} fent
for me and told me he would have
no other fees taken than fuch as
were directed by Ordinance, for tho'
there was feveral Perfons named in
the Act Yet it was no more than
one. I obferved to his Ex^{cy} that

when the Committee met upon that
Act they were of opinion that each
Perfon named therein in paying
20*f.* to the Secretary was but reafonable; he faid he had nothing to
do with their private opinion and
with fome heat fay'd, you had never
acquainted him of it, and moreover
he lookt upon y^t demand to be an
Exaction, and that I might acquaint
you of the fame.

I will obferve your good cautions
and any . . . . . . *Coden* brings
news from *Rhode Ifland* y^t twenty
three of the Pyrates are Condemn'd
there, one ordered for Execution,
Capt. *Solgard* was to fail from there
Sunday laft.

Inclofed is four pound.

Iſaac Bobin to George Clarke.

July yᵉ 19ᵗʰ 1723.

Honᵈ Sir

I HAVE received your Letter of
Yeſterday that you therein mention of Saturday laſt did not come
to hand before Wedneſday laſt, and
to which I then ſent you an anſwer
by *Guyon Neſbit*, The ſubſtance
thereof being that Mr. *Wileman* has
Mr. *Byerly's* Mortgage in order to
make Oath to the Execution of it.

That I have ſpoke to *Lawrence*
who has promiſed me to uſe his
Beſt Endeavours to get a Maid
Servant for you.

That I delivered your Letter to
the Treaſurer.

That the Governour will not al-
low any more fees to be taken or

received for the naturalization Acts
than what is directed by Ordinance,
and now in confequence of yours of
yefterday I have been at Mr. *Laws*
to acquaint him that *Will* had loft
the Letter from him to you but he
is gone out of Town.

The Treafurer defires to be
excufed from writing by this Opportunity by reafon he is now very
bufy making up his accounts.

I have paid *John Smith* forty fhillings and fend inclofed in fmall
Bills four pounds.

The Acts of Affembly now paft
I believe will be fent home by the
Snow that is expected dayly here
with *Franks*.

Yefterday in the Evening arrived
here from *Briftoll* after a Paffage of
Nine weeks I do not hear that fhe
brings any news.

S

Ripet is likewife arrived from
Barbados but has brought no fruit.
I am with refpect
Sᵣ your &c.
I BOBIN.

Mifs *Molly* is very well.

Ifaac Bobin to George Clarke.

SECRETARY'S OFFICE, NEW YORK,
July yᵉ 27ᵗʰ 1723.

Honᵈ Sir

I HAVE received yours of Yefterday; according to your defire
therein I have been with the Treafurer who tells me his Accounts will
be ready for you on Thurfday or
Friday next.

Inclofed is four pounds in fmall
Bills.

I fend now by *Will* two pᵣ of

Traces @ 5*f*, 4*d*; Leading Lines
3*f*. 4½*d*; twelve pound of ftarch
6*f*.; Three Yards of White filk
Galloon 1*f*. 6*d*; Padlock and fta-
ples 3*f*.

I have writ this morning to Mr.
Thos Dongan by an Opportunity
that offered for *Staten Ifland*.

I will mind *Lawrence* of what
you write me concerning a Dairy
Maid and Red Clover feed.

Capt *Solgard* arrived here on
Thurfday laft; after Careening his
fhip he defigns to take another
Cruife,

Capt. *Jarratt* is not yet arrived.

I. BOBIN.

Mr. *Clarke.*

Isaac Bobin to George Clarke.

SECRETARY'S OFFICE, NEW YORK,
Auguſt yᵉ 1ſt 1723.

Honᵈ Sir

I HAVE received your Letter of Yeſterday by *Will*, and ſend now by him a Barrˡ of Beef at 37ſ. 6d bought at Mr. *Jay's*. I am In-form'd by the Packers 'tis the beſt in Town, Mr. *Jay* ſays he'll warrant it to be good, I ſend likewiſe the Candle Box with Candles qᵗ 75 pᵈ at 7½d ℔ pᵈ as alſo a Bits-worth of Allum ; The other things I will ſend by *Riche;* every thing bought for your uſe is with this Caution if not likt either as to 'tis price or goodneſs to be taken again ; this I do to prevent deceit, and will obſerve the hint you·give me concerning

Mr. *Alexander*. The Galloon I fent laft was not bought there, but at Mrs. *Stillwells*, who upon writing to her about the Extraordinary price of the Galloon fent me the inclofed anfwer and fays fhe pays half a bit a yard for it at the Merchants by the p⁵ and that all fhe had left fhe fold at the price of that fhe fold you.

I have paid *Elenor Carpenter* your note in her favour.

I am glad to hear you have received no damage from the ftorm we have had laft Monday it has done confiderable to the Docks.

The inclofed Letter I believe to be from Mr. *Thomas Dongan* in anfwer to what I writ him.

The Treafurer's Accounts are ready.

The Mafter of a *Briftoll* Veffell has been fo kind to prefent me with

a Bottle of Capers which I defire
you'll accept from   Sʳ
           Your humble Servant
                    I. Bobin.
Geo. *Clarke* Efq.

Thomas Dongan to Ifaac Bobin.

      Sʳ

I WAS favour'd wᵗʰ yours this
 Morning relateing to Mr. *Clarke's*
affairs and herewith fend him an
anfwer. I fhould be glad if leifure
did permit to have the fatisfaction
of feeing yᵘ at my Houfe, and fhall
be allways proud if any opportunity
offers wherein I can fhow my fincere
acknowledgmᵗ of the favours con-
ferr'd by you upon   Sʳ
      Your oblig'd humble
                    Servᵗ
           Thoˢ Dongan.

Ifaac Bobin to Robert King.

SECRETARY'S OFFICE, NEW YORK,
Septr ye 11th 1723.

Sir

MR. Secretary *Clarke* being in want of a Negro wench & I having had advice from Mr. *King* that there is one to be fold at *Amboy* on a months Likeing, before I mention it to Mr. *Clarke* I fhould be glad to know the reafon of her being fold and whether upon Enquiry you may think fhe is fit for fervice and that no ill qualitys attend her.

Sr I have very little acquaintance at *Amboy* is the occafion of my giving you this trouble defiring you'll be fo kind to make fuch an Inquiry and to let me hear from you concerning yᶜ fame fo foon as conveniently may be; I muſt confeſs I can't conclude without bluſhing for my freedom herein.

Iſaac Bobin to George Clarke.

SECRETARY'S OFFICE, N. YORK,

Sept. 14*th* 1723.

Hon^d Sir

SINCE my Letter to you of Yeſterday by *Riche* I have received yours of the ſame day. All the things mentioned in your Memorandum are a Board of *Riche*. *Riche* not being gone *Will* takes the ſmall things with him. Mrs. *Schuyler* now ſends a p^s of Shalone, a p^s of Muſlin & a p^s of Linen Silk. She adviſes me to acquaint you that ſhe cant get a p^s of Druget in Town to match the ſhalone under forty yards.

Sr The weather not being fetled, I have not ventur'd to fend the Papers.

As to Mifs *Mollys* Trunk &^{a} Mrs. *Congreve* will take care to fend in fuch order as they may goe fafe. Mr. *Cook* fays the Spinnet muft not go till the Weather is better fettled, & y^t he will tune it and Quil it as likewife fet her fome Tunes. *Will* Informs me of Mad^m C—— being brought to Bed of a girl of which I give you Joy and am

The Council will fet to Morrow, in order to fign ye quarterly Warrants & to receive ye Report of ye Com^{ee} upon ye Computation.

The Govr has named the prefent Mayor & Sheriff of this City to be Mayor & Sheriff for the year Enfuing; he has likewife made no alteration at *Albany* in the Majeftrates; will go for *Jerfey* Monday next.

T

I have fent a few Limes wch I defire you'll pleafe to accept with my hearty wifhes for Mad^m *Clarkes* recovery, I am glad Mr. *Riggs* prevailed upon Mr. *Brown* to go with *Will* and am with all due regard.

S^r   Yours &c.

Ifaac Bobin to George Clarke.

SECRETARY'S OFFICE, NEW YORK,
Septemb. ye 15th 1723.

Hon^d Sir

THERE goes now by *Riche* (upon whom I could not prevail to go fooner) a Barrel of Beef £1. 17ƒ. 6d; a Q^r Cafk of Wine @ £6 ; twelve pound of hard Soap @ 6ƒ; twelve p^d of Chocolat £1. 1ƒ; two Barr^ls of Beer a p^d of Bohea Tea @ £1.; Six q^r of writing

(147)

Paper. *Will* carryed with him from Mr. *Lanes* four Bottles of Brandy with a Letter from Mr. *Lane.*

I have not fent Mifs *Mollys* Spinnet, Mr. *Cook* telling me it would be fpoilt if fent in wet Weather; he has promifed me to Tune it to day or to morrow; the Frame &^{c} referred till another time by reafon of ye weather.

Yefterday I laid before his Ex^{cy} in Council according to order the Treafurers Accounts, together with your Computation of the Auditor's fees for Auditting the fame. Whereupon his Excellency referred it to the Gent. of the Council or any five of them to Examine. whether the Computation of the Auditor's Salary be right, I acquainted him with ye Reafon of your fo fuddenly leaving the Town.

Robert King to Ifaac Bobin.

PERTH AMBOY, *Septembr* 24th 1723.

Sir

PURSUANT to Mr. *Thomas Dunckans* requeſt have inquired for a Negro Wench whither ſhe may ſute Mr. Sec^{try} *Clarks* Service I know not —

but that ſhe hath bin in this Country ab^t three years hath a healthy Like man Childe of ab^t Eight mo: ould; I believe will be ſould for 50 or 51 *l* her want of being well taught is the only objection I make ſhe hath but Lately faln into propper hands was my ſervant near two years, the dutty Negros are ſubjeċt to at *N: York* I find will make the owner ſcruple ſending her in caſe it be required untill that be Clear'd, tho' tis likely

that doᶜᵗʳ *Hume* pᵈ it when he
imported her wᵗʰ other Negros
pleaſs to favour me with your an-
ſware that I may Let the owner
of the Servᵗ know, with my moſt
humble reſpeᴄts to Mr. *Clarke,*
Sir Your moſt Humble Servᵗ

ROBᵀ KING.

Iſaac Bobin to George Clarke.

SECRY'S OFFICE, NEW YORK,
September yᵉ 28ᵗʰ 1723.

Honᵈ Sir,

THE Drugget &c. from Mr.
Schuyler is ready to go by *Riche*
as well as Miſs *Molly's* Spinnet.
Mr. *Cook* promiſed me ſome New
Tunes for her but is gone without
giving me any.—

I have not heard from *Amboy*
about Mr. *King's* Wench but will
write again.

I have been with Mrs. *Vernon* concerning *Windiford's* Negro Wench,
who tells me fhe muft have a further
Tryall of her before fhe can give
her Opinion; The Wench goes
there again Monday next for further
Tryal.

Coll. *Lurting* has not any of your
damnifyed flannen left, Mr. *Lane*
informs me that he has fent Mr.
Chifwells Bills for you by Mr.
Bickley.

Franks informs me the Veffel he
came in from *London* will not fail
for that place before the middle of
next Month. I have paid Mr.
Brownell for Mifs *Mollys* fchooling
as likewife for Six Balls of Gold &
one of Silver Thread for Mifs *Molly*,
at £1. 6f. which I fend now by
Mr. *Winman* the Upholfterer. The
bearer being impatient to go will
give me time to add nothing more.

Isaac Bobin to George Clarke.

SECRETARY'S OFFICE, NEW YORK,
Octobr y*e* 1*st* 1723.

Hon^d Sir

I HAVE received yours of Yes-terday by good Mr. *Bickley*, and will be carefull in sending Miss *Mollys* Spinnet &c^a by *Riche*, with the other things you write for.

I have writ again to *Amboy*.

Sr Upon hearing that Doctor *Dupuy* had a Negro Wench to dispose of I have spoke to him concerning her who tells me the Attorney General and some others are about buying her, but you shall have the preference, he is willing to let her go upon Tryal for a Month, not doubting but you'll find her a good slave, She is about Nineteen and twenty Years of age brought up in his Family from an Enfant, he will not take lefs for her than fifty five pounds. Mrs. *Harding* fent a White woman Servant to me with the inclofed Note who fays She is willing to ferve you if you have occafion, That fhe underftands any thing belonging to Houfehold affairs y^t fhe and her hufband is come from *Bofton* where they had a fmall Settlement in the Country but the Indians having deftroyed which reduced them to look for a livelyhood, her hufband likewife offers his fervices if you have occafion, he tells me he has been brought up to Agriculture Hufbandry and that he likewife underftands Weaving, They are people about thirty years of age Sturdy and ftrong and feem well made to work —

I have fpoke to *Lawrence* con-

cerning the Clover feed who has
promifed me very faithfully to bring
it next Trip—

As to the Lawyers Accounts Mr.
Wileman has taken the Minutes of
the Supream Court from me in
order to make them out, he fhewed
me that he has begun upon them,
and fays that he will fet all bufinefs
afide to Compleat them, I told
him that he had fo often made fuch
promifes that you had no hopes of
his ever compleating them, and that
I would do them, in Anfwer to
which he told me no one could do
them fo well as himfelf they having
been taken in his time, and y^t he
fhould be as uneafy as yourfelf till
they were done.

Since I writ this I have received
yours by *Will*, and fend now by
him —— of Candles, an hour Glafs
1 ʃ 6*d* a pound of Bohea Tea £1 ;

V

half a hundred of Gun Flint 2ʃ 6d
and four yards and three Nailes of
yᵈ Wide Flannen, & 8 pᵈ of Hops.
As to Hemp Seed I have Enquired
of Capt *Searl* who tells me he has
not any, nor does not know of any
in Town, but that he has writ to
Jerſey for ſome and if he gets any
will ſpare me as much as you deſire.
As to Miſs *Mollys* muſick it will go
with the Spinnot. The things from
Mrs. *Schuyler* go likewiſe with *Will*,
Mrs. *Schuyler* has thought fit to
ſend the whole piece of Drugget
and what remains ſhe take back.

Isaac Bobin to George Clarke.

Secry's Office, New York,
Octobr ye 16th 1723.

Hon^d Sir

I HAVE received your Letter of yesterday and have paid *Nurse Parker* five pounds and send inclosed in Small Bills, three pounds.

The several sundarys sent by *Will* are mentioned in the within memo. with their prices. I have ventur'd to buy a pair of stockings over and above the number mentioned in your Letter *Will* telling me he is very much in want of a pair, and that he had forgot to speak to you otherwise they wou'd have been mentioned in the Letter, As to ye scales &c. they must go by next Opportunity the Man not having got them ready according to promise.

The pˢ of Linen from Mrs. *Schuy-*
ler I am afraid is too Coarſe but
ſhe tells me ſhe has no other yᵗ
comes near the price you deſired as
yᵗ now ſent yᵉ price being £3. 8ſ.
her Family is very much out of
Order and deſires to be excuſed if
ſhe cannot doe as ſhe could wiſh.

Mr. *Kennedy* tells me the Quit
Rents come in ſo ſlow that he has
very little Caſh in hand but if 9 or
10 pounds will be of any ſervice he
will advance it on Credit of the
Warrant.

Bradford has not any of *Lillys* Accedences or Accedences and Grammars, but expeᴄts ſome dayly from
Boſton as well as *Philadelphia* —

The Letters you ſent to the
Treaſurers I have Copy'd ſeal'd and
delivered to him, who tells me he
is indiſpoſed with the Feaver inſo-
much that he is not able to take

Pen in hand to make anſwer to it
but ſo ſoon as he is better will.

The Clover ſeed goes now by
Will as likewiſe Mr. *Dupuys* Negro
Wench, I could not prevail upon
her maſter to give her two Blankets
ſo have bought her a couple according to order, he has given her a pair
of New Shoes and Stockins.

I underſtand ſhe does not want
for Cloſe, ſhe is unwilling to be
ſold, and her Miſtreſs as unwilling
to part from her, which makes the
D[r] afraid ſhe'll be ſtuborn and ſay
ſhe can do nothing but deſires you'll
not believe her for ſhe can do every
thing belonging to a Houſe, except
milking a Cow, She has liv'd ſome
time with Mr. *Nicholls* the Poſt
Maſter which made me Inquire of
him as to her Character who tells
me ſhe is a Wench knows the buſineſs of a Houſe, but that who ever

buys her muſt have a watchful Eye
over her otherwiſe ſhe will be apt
to Idle her time. I have enquired
at other places where ſhe has liv'd
but do not hear an Ill Character of
her, I hope ſhe may anſwer to Ex-
pectation.

The Veſſell for *London* will ſail
next week.

I can't get any Spaniſh Tobacco
but have ſent all I had in the Office
and am with reſpect

Sir
Your moſt obedient
humble Servant
I BOBIN.

(159)

Iſaac Bobin to George Clarke.

SECRETARY'S OFFICE, NEW YORK,
Octobr yᵉ 21ſt 1723.

Honᵈ Sir

AT the requeſt of Mr. *Haſkoll* I
ſend you the incloſed by the
bearer (who is paid for his Journey
by the Governour) —

I ſend you by this opportunity Mr.
Byerlys Bond & Mortgage which I
have Recorded and Examined.

Capᵗ *Solgard* arrived here yeſterday from his Cruiſe.

I hear they have done very little
as yet in *Jerſey*. That ſince the
Governour has been there they have
had but one Council, and the Aſſembly have Reſolved to ſtrike Bills
of Credit to the Value of forty
thouſand pounds the one half to be
Proclamation and the other half to

bear the Credit of *New York* Currency; the whole to be funk in 20
years.

I met laft Saturday *Andrew John-
fton* who told me the reafon of not
anfwering my Letter was his coming
to Town that he had enquired as
to y^c Ch. of the Negro Wench to
be difpofed of at *Amboy*, that he is
informed fhe is ftuborn & not very
active at her work, that fhe belongs
to one *Harrifon* who was formerly
Sheriff of *Amboy*, and the only
reafon of her being fold is the want
of money—The price he tells is
Seventy five pounds for her and her
Child about four years of age which
I look on to be a very extraordinary
price, efpecially for one that has
not being long in the Country, and
knows but little as he tells me. I
hope *Dupuy's* Wench will pleafe
Mad^m *Clarke*, fo if you believe fhe

will not do I ſhould be glad to
know that I may Inquire further
and am

Iſaac Bobin to George Clarke.

SECRETARY'S OFFICE, NEW YORK,

Octob. yᵉ 29ᵗʰ 1723.

Honᵈ Sir

I HAVE received yours of Yeſterday by *Will* and ſend now by
him the ſeveral particulars mentioned in the incloſed Memorandum,
The other things I will endeavor to
get ready to go by *Riche.*

I have incloſed four Pounds, &
have given *Will* 22ſ. to buy a Hatt
at the Ferry for your Carpenter.

The bearer arrived here Saturday
laſt from *London* after a Paſſage of
Six weeks—The *Sunderland* was to
follow him in Six days after he

W

Sailed, and the Ship *Samuel* in ten,
Captain *Symes* is Confirmd as likewife *Blood* who is Commanded up
to *Albany*, and young Mr. *Riggs* is
to take his Poft here—As to News
I begg leave to referr you to y^e
inclofed Papers which Mr. *Delancey*
has been fo kind to give me.

The inclofed Letters I received
from Mr. *Nicholls* except one which
I believe to be from Mr. *Dongan*.

Ifaac Bobin to George Clarke.

SECRETARY'S OFFICE, NEW YORK,
November ye 13th 1723.

Hon^d Sir

I HAVE received yours of Yefterday by *Will*, I have been at
Dr. *Dupuys* but have not feen him
but expect to fee him fome time to
Day I will then mention to him

what you write me concerning
Mary, I believe it will be neceſſary
to take a Bill of Sale for her when
the Money is paid. —

Capt *Low* won't Let the Boy go
on Tryal. —

Meſſ^rs *Schuyler* and *Van Brugh*
tell me they can not now inform
me of what you deſire but will be
particular in ſending an anſwer by
ye Poſt to every thing after they
arrive at *Albany,* The Deed they
have carryed with them in order to
be Executed there by Coll *Jno Syl-
veſter.* I incloſe you Mr. *Van Dams*
Memorandum of the Account relating to *Schohare* thoſe Gentlemen
have been very Extravigant in their
Account, in one Article they charged
twenty five pounds for y^t Expence
and fatiague of their Voyage from
Albany, which Article is ſtruck out
as well as ſome others which Mr.

Van Dam look'd upon to be very Exhorbitant. Mr. *Kennedy* has paid me £15. on account of your Warrant of Incidents which fum is inclofed, and he was juft then going for *Amboy* fo that he had not time to fill up the Blanks in the Account of Mr. *Walpoles* Horfe.

I have received from Mr. *Bickley* 44 Ounces & a half of Silver at 9*ſ* ℔ Ounce.—The *Beaver* will faile the twentyeth of this Inftant— *Bradford* has not yet got any of *Lillys* accidences or Grammars he has promifed to let me know when they come As to flax I have not yet inquired for any Expecting that Mr. *Dongan* in his Letters to you might have given you an account of fome, but have fent £1. pᵈ for prefent ufe. I will now Enquire for that as well as Hemp feed I cannot get any Spanifh Tobacco good enough to fend now, but will fee further againft next opportunity.

The fhip *Sunderland* arrived here monday laft, after a Paffage of 7 weeks from ye *Lizard* Capt *Symes* is come with his Commiffion for Captain; the King was expected home ye 2^d of October.

There was not any Letters for you in the Poft Office; that for Mad^m *Hyde* I had from Mr. *Nicholls*.

Mr. *Cook* has fent feveral Wires that Mifs *Molly* may take which fhe thinks will fuit Beft, he tells me that he is very forry Mifs has left the Town for that fhe will forget all fhe has Learnt; he propofes to go to the *Plains* fome time next week, but fays he cant confine himfelf to the Country above a Day; he defired me prefent his humble fervices to yourfelf Mad^m *Clarke* Mad^m *Hyde* and Mifs *Molly*,

Molly Decan defired me likewife to mention yᵗ fhe Joyns therein. I fend now by *Will* with the other things mentioned in yᵉ jnclofed memorandum a few Limes which I hope you'll accept from

Sʳ

&c.

I. BOBIN.

Mr. *Clarke.*

C. Denne to Ifaac Bobin.

DEN HILL, *noubr* yᶜ 14. 1723.

Kind Sʳ

I RECEUED yours dated oᶜᵗʳ yᶜ 30 : I mett with the doctors man & *beats* together I Red. that Letter to *beats* as you writte to him & alfo Repremanded him ffor Giuen the Doctors Land an ill Report ; he has promifed me that he will not

doe foe no more ffor the time to
Come the docters man was uery
well fatisffied and told to me that
beats would go off without any
ffurther trouble S^r I fhall always
be Redy to ferue you or yours when
I haue Refeued foe many ffauours
ffrom & hope I fhall Liuee to make
you amends ffor, which I haue not
yet done.

S^r I now make bold to trouble
you with a Line or to ffor to Lett
you know that our good neighbours
haue been a plotting againft me
again there is that white Lookt
Gent *John Everett* and *duning* has
made it theire hole bufnefs to fett
Juftice *Alfup* and my felfe at uarence
which is at a uery hie degree & alfoe
againft Judge *Blagg* & old Mr.
Clowes S^r I pray pardon me ffor it
is to Long to much ffor to give you
the hole acompt but If you fhould

fee Judge *Blagg* he will in fform to
you the hole matter S^r my feruice
to your felfe & to Docter *Dupuy* &
to my Good ffrind *John Chambers*
whoe is with Refpect
　Your ffrind & humble ferv^t
　　　　　　　C. Denne.

Ifaac Bobin to George Clarke.

Novr ye 22^d 1723.

Hon^d Sir

I HAVE received yours of the 18th
jnft, and am glad to hear you
have hopes the fervant I fent will
do ; after copying and fealing *Lawrence Smyth's* Letter I have fent it
under Cover to Mr. *Andrew John-
fon* defiring him to forward it ; all
the Papers you fent me I fend now
back by this Opportunity fairly
Copyed and Examined.

(169)

The Letters you fent for *England*
I have put into the *Beaver's* Bagg —
The Treafurer continues much in-
difpofed fo that he does not know
when he fhall be able to get his
Accounts ready — I fend herewith
20*l* of 22^d nails and fix q^r of Copying
Paper.

I will obferve what you write me
concerning Mr. *Van Dam*, When
Riche comes I will fend by him
The Candles and Chocolate and the
Charrot Wheels if they be ready.

I am

S^r

&c.

I. BOBIN.

X

Iſaac Bobin to George Clarke.

SECRETARY's OFF., N. YORK,

Novembr yͤ 27ᵗʰ 1723.

Honᵈ Sir

I SEND now by *Riche* a Box of Candles and am ſorry thoſe I ſent before of Mrs. *Smiths* prov'd ſo bad, thoſe that go now I have bought at one *Peltreau* where I was jnform'd they were better. As to the Chocolate it is ſo dear I have not ſent any the loweſt they aſk is two and nine pence the pound and that but very Indifferent Cocoa being ſold at 10 & 11 pounds the hundred.

Sunday laſt arrived here the ſhip *Samuel* from *London* the 23ᵈ of September and from the *Downs* the 29ᵗʰ It is Believed ſhe will ſail from hence in about 10 or fourteen days the greateſt part of her loading being ready — Mr. *Sharpas* prefents his humble Service to you and Mad^m *Clarke* as likewife to Mad^m *Hyde* and Mifs *Molly* in wch I beg leave to Join and has defired me to fend you the inclofed Political ftates for the Months of July and Auguft laft.

The Treafurer continues ftill jn-difpofed.

We are not yet upon any certainty when the Governour will come from *Jerfey*.

I have not yet heard from Mr. *Smith* of *Amboy*.

Yours &c.
I. BOBIN.

Iſaac Bobin to George Clarke.

SECRETARY'S OFFICE, NEW YORK,

Dec. yᵉ 6ᵗʰ 1723.

Honᵈ Sir

IT was laſt night before I recᵈ yours of the 23ᵈ paſt by *Riche*— I have ſent you the Papers therein mentioned fairly Copyed by Mr. *Lawrence* which I hope you have received.

Mr. *Wileman* tells me has near compleated the Lawyers accᵗˢ I ſend now by *Riche* a pound of Bohea Tea £1. 9ſ an ou of Blew ſewing ſilk 4ſ 6.

The *Sunderland* is bound this Trip for *Jamaica*, We have no other Veſſell going for *London* but the *Samuel* which will ſail the Latter End of next week.

Mrs. *Patty Ludlow* having not

time to go with me to buy y^c
Huckaback you write for and *Riche*
being in hafte to go it muft therefore be fent by next opportunity.

Coll *Riggs* defires me to prefent
his humble fervice to you Mad^m
and Mad^m *Hyde*.

Ifaac Bobin to George Clarke.

SECRETARY'S OFFICE, NEW YORK,

January ye 7th 1723.

Hon^d Sir

I HAVE received yours of the 4th
Inftant, and fend now the feveral
particulars mentioned in the inclofed
memorandum.

The wine I hope you'll find
good — it is bought of *Jno Vanhorn*
where Mr. *Sharpas* had is, I cou'd
not prevail upon him to fpare a
Hogfhead —

George Burnet has not any Blew
Stockings at 9*f.* a p^r left, but has
fent two p^r of Blew at 10*f.* and the
Purple and Green @ 9*f.* as likewife
a p^r of coarfe @ 6*f.* he is willing
not to be paid for them before he
knows whether Mad^m *Clarke* likes
them. I fend you Mrs. *Schuylers* Accounts and the Key of the Trunk,
The Enrollment of all the Laws
fince the Governours arrival is per-
fected & I will obferve what you
write me in taking a fair opportunity
of getting a Warrant for that Service
as well as for Incidents and the Rent
Roll.

The Govr & Council has appointed
Dr. *Colden* Surveyor and Commif-
fioner with Mr. *Harifon* Coll *Pro-
vooft* and Mr. *Janfen* or any 3 of
them to meet on the 1st Tuefday in
February next at *Rye*, the Com^{rs}
to be appointed by *Connecticut* for

running the Line between this Province and that Colony.

I have given *Will* Eighteen pence
to pay for mending *Molly Shepards*
ſhoes.

Mr. *Wileman* tells me he has near
finiſhed the Lawyers Bills and is
now going on in order to compleat
them.

Mr. *Kennedy* has paid me the
Ballance of your account which I
ſend herewith together with the
Receipts you deſire, and a Letter
from him. Incloſed is a Letter
from *England* by the way of *Boſton*,
The Veſſell arriv'd brings no news
worthy Notice.

I ſend incloſed the *Boſton* & *Philadelphia* Papers of laſt Poſt.

The Smith yᵗ mended your Jack
was imployed by one *Robin* a Braſier
to whom *Will* gave it for mending,
the Smith is gone to the Country

and the Brafier tells me he paid him 6*f.* for mending of it but that fince it fo happens y^t it will not doe he will not charge it.

I have not heard from the Man that promifed me the Flaxfeed. I will Enquire further.

I heartily wifh you a happy New Year and many others with Mad^m *Clarke* and your good family. The Guns go back mended as likewife the Jack, I am

Yours
I Bobin.

Memorandum of Sundrys fent by Will
January ye 7th 172⅞.

12 ℔ of hard Soap at *Pelte-*
　　reau Senr　　　　£0. 6. 0
1^l of Bohea Tea at Mrs.
　　Kierfteds　　　　0. 19. 0
1 Quarter Cafk of Wine at
　　Mr. *John Vanhorne*　7. 0. 0

A pair of white Girls fhoes £o. 6. o
Negro fhoes   o. 5. 6
Tacks   o. 2. o
Yeft   o. o. 9
Five pair of ftockings from
   George Burnet   2. 4. o

Ifaac Bobin to George Clarke.

SECRETARY'S OFFICE, NEW YORK,
March yᶜ 3ᵈ 172⅞.

Honᵈ Sir,

I HAVE received yours of the 13ᵗʰ paft by *Riche* the feveral particulars mentioned in the inclofed memorandum go now by him, The doz. of Bos Combs and Comb Brufh Mrs. *Clarke* was fo kind to take with her. I can not meet with a pair of kidd gloves of a fize fit for Mifs *Molly*, nor a large kitchen knife; I have fent all the filk I could get near the Pattern fent.

Y

I will Enquire for Garden Beans
and fpeak to Mr. *DeLancey* for fome
Goofberry Trees.

I fend. you a few Limes which I
defire you'll pleafe to accept. I
have put 'em in a little Bagg and
feald it to prevent *Riche* taking toll
as he calls it, & have y^c promife of
more to morrow with fome Oranges
which I will put afide again to next
opportunity of fending.

Mr. *Bickley* and Mad^m *Bickley*
are come to ftay at their Houfe in
Town till after the Supreame Court,
Mr. *Bickley* being very weak but is
now upon y^c mending hand, they
both prefent their humble fervice
to you and Mad^m *Clarke* as likewife
Mifs *Hyde*. I have written a third
letter about the Flax —

(179)

A List of Sundarys sent by Riche March
3ᵈ 172¾ *viz*ᵗ

	£	s	d
Three pound of Chocolate	£0.	7.	6
One yᵈ of stuff	0.	2.	6
One oz & ½ of Sowing silk scarce wᵗ but is all that could be got			
31 Gal. of Molasses @ 1 *s*. 10 *d*	2.	16.	0
pound of Bohea Tea	0.	18.	0
Three sheets of Minikin Pins	0.	3.	0
Three Blue Laces	0.	5.	0

If yᵉ prices of any of the above particulars are not liked they will be taken again.

Iſaac Bobin to George Clarke.

S. OFFICE, NEW YORK,
March 14ᵗʰ 172⅞.

Honᵈ Sir,

I HAVE received yours of yᵉ 10ᵗʰ Inſtant by Mr. *Lawrence* and am glad the little fruit I ſent met with your kind acceptance. I ſend you ſome Tobacco.

I have ſent you a Taſt of old *Burnets* Tea at 8ſ. a pound its ſome that he bought at Vendue & I am jnformed is damaged, brought here by *Hickford* the Privateer, I am ſorry Mrs. *Bergen* has diſappointed Madᵐ *Clarke*, but I will Enquire elſe where.

The Coach maker has better than half finiſhed the Wheels, and tells me they had been done before now had not one of his Men fallen fick but will fee to get them done out of hand.

I fend you inclofed five pounds in fmall Bills, We have had two very dead quarters for bufinefs of the Office but hope it will be brifker. I fend you fome Salecia Lettice feed, Cabbage Lettice feed, and Sellery feed as much of every fort as I could get, as likewife five quarts of Beans, being all the Man would fpare, having promifed fome to Mr. *De-Lancey.*

Mr. *DeLancey* tells me the Goofberry Trees are ready at half a hours warning.

Inclofed is a letter from Mr. *Phillipfe* concerning Mrs. *Hegeman.* I have omitted to acquaint you that the governour approves of your thoughts of admonifhing Mr. *Phillipfe* the Diffenting Minifter and

directed me to send him a Letter
of admonition accordingly.

Mr. *Bickley* last night was taken
with a Bleeding of the Nose, but is
better to day, he purposes to pay
you a visit after a Supream Court is
over and stay for some time retired.

I am sorry to hear you have
sprained your hand. The Governour will go for *Jerseys* the Beginning
of next Month.—I am &c.

I. BOBIN.

Isaac Bobin to George Clarke.

SECRETARY'S OFFICE, NEW YORK,
June the 8th 1724.

Hon^d Sir,

I HAVE had the happyness of
seeing Madam *Clarke* and re-
ceiving her Commands—She has
had Six pounds and Miss *Molly* four
Dollars.

I will obferve what you write me
concerning *Cook ;* Mifs has been fo
kind to promife to let me know the
Day fhe begins.

I will endeavour to get fuch Cyder as you defire —

Madam *Clarke* has a pound of
Bohea Tea, as to Ink powder there
is none in Town.

I fend you inclofed the Votes from
the firft of this jnftant to the fourth ;
a Committee of ye Houfe have fince
Reported that they had Examined
the accounts of the Treafurer and
find that the Colony on the 13 of
this jnftant will be in arrear the fum
of £3721. 15. 7½ 'tis believed they
will go upon the *Jerfey* projeét in
raifing of Money to the value of
one hundred or four fcore thoufand
pounds this is what they talk off
over a glafs of Wine at the widdow
Poft's, but nothing as yet has been

motion'd in the Houſe relating thereto.

They will ſtrike New Bills of Credit in the Room of the old.

I will be carefull in giving you timely notice of every thing that may be in agitation.

Ludlow tells me it will be a fort-night or three weeks before there will be any buſineſs for the Council. I have done what you deſired con-cerning *Sarah Tudor*.

Johnſon for *Holland* ſayl'd this day —

I am &c.

Iſaac Bobin to George Clarke.

S. Off^z New York,
June ye 18th 1724.

Hon^d Sir

I HAVE received yours of yeſ-terday by *Cæſar*, The Chariot Wheels and Boards are ready to go by *Riche* I will in the mean time get the Lynſeed Oyl and what elſe is wanting, as to Cyder I cannot find any in Town that I dare venture upon. There goes now by *Cæſar* twelve pound of Soap and pair of Childs ſhoes with four pounds four ſhillings in Dollars—

The affair of Mr. *Dublois* I will ſee to adjuſt.

Miſs *Molly* is very well.

Madam *Bickley* yeſterday proved Mr. *Bickley's* Will.

Myndert Schuyler Yeſterday took his place in the Aſſembly in the Room of *Hanſen;* he tells me he jntends to pay you a viſit next week having ſomething to offer which he believes will be very much for your and his advantage.

Z

Ifaac Bobin to George Clarke.

SECRETARY'S OFFICE, NEW YORK,
June yᵉ 27ᵗʰ 1724.

Honᵈ Sir

I HAVE received this morning yours of Yefterday by *Will.* I have been at the Treafurers but he was not at home. I will go there again for his anfwer to what you defire and let you know when his accounts will be ready to audit.

The feveral particulars mentioned in the inclofed memorandum go by *Will* with an acᵗ of thofe that could not be got.

The Affembly have not done any thing worthy of notice fince my laft—The money to be levyed for repair of the Garrifon they have Refolved to raife upon a Land Tax.

Mr. *Harifon* is appointed Recorder of this City in the Room of Mr. *Jamifon*.

The Chairott Wheels and Planks are gone by *Riche*.

I fend fix pair of Gloves for Mad^m *Clarke*; thefe for Mifs *Molly* I have fent to Mrs. *Vernons*.

Capt. *Solgard* arrived yefterday from *Virginia* he gave me the inclofed for forwarding to you — inclofed is ten Dollars.

I will remember what you write me concerning old *Burnet*:

. I wifh you a good harveft and am with all due regard S^r

&c.

Iſaac Bobin to George Clarke.

Honᵈ Sir,

I SEND you by *Goodwin* a Hogſhead of Madera which I hope
will prove to content, I have been
carefull to get a good Hogſhead to
put it in, but wiſh the drawing it
off from the Pipe to the Hogſhead
may not alter its Body. Mr. *Read*
was willing I ſhould take the Pipe
but did not know what to do without your order.

Madᵐ *Burnet* was brought bedd
this morning off a ſon.

I have been very uneaſy at the
Coach makers changing the boxes
of your Charrott Wheels & have
ſent him a Threatning Letter which
I hope may bring them to light.

(189)

The fellow to whom I paid the
Money for him fwears they are
the fame that were brought from
the *Plains*, but I believe him to be
a Rogue like the other.

I am glad you met with better
weather on Saturday than you expected and am

I have delivered your Letter to
Mr. *Le Heup.*

John Rochead to Ifaac Bobin.

JAMAICA, *ffryday night* 172⅘.

Dr Ifaac

I HAVE fent by the Bearer *Thomas
Brown* a filver hilted fword which
pleafe deliver to Capt *Andrew Nicoll*
of your fort and receive nine pounds
for it; the fpair fcabbard he fhall
have when I come to Town.

Pleafe forward the Inclofed for *Edinburgh* in yours to Mr. *Willard* in *Bofton;* you need not inclofe it in that to your father but lett him put yours and it into the firft fhips Bagg bound for *London, Briftol* &c.

I defyre you would get heavy gold (if it is not to much trouble) for the fword money I defign to fee the Secretary's family on Munday if you have any Commands thither lett me have them by the Bearer.

Give Sir *George Oglevie's* Note to Mr. *Jamifon* jun^r to fue & if you want a power to do it fhall fend him one—Your new Major *W*—— here is dangeroufly Ill. *Jamie* gives his fervice to you and landlord, as does

Your moft hearty humble S^t

JOHN ROCHEAD.

Tho: Brown did not go to Town till Wenfday & then fhall fend ye fword.

Iſaac Bobin to Govʳ Burnet.

May it pleaſe yoʳ Excellency

I HAVE received yoʳ Exᶜʸˢ Lre with yᵗ of Capᵗ *Barnaret's* to yʳ Excellency and accordingly prepared a Warrant for the Auditting and adjuſting The ſeveral Accᵗˢ of Diſburſements for Careening his Majeſty's ſhip under his Command as well as to Enquire into the preſent Currency of Exchange for Bills drawn by him on the Navy which I ſend herewith.

I am obliged by this Opportunity to give your Excellency the trouble of ſome Blank Let Paſſes wᶜʰ I deſire you'll be pleaſed to ſign and ſeal.

The incloſed Letters were given me Yeſterday by one Monſieur *Rameſay* the Governours Son of *Mountreall*

for forwarding to your Excellency,
he is under much concern for the
Seal of one of them being broke by
Accident in his Pocket & has defired
me to acquaint you y^t he hopes your
Excellency will Entertain a better
opinion of him than to believe he
has toucht the Seal; he very much
wifhed for ye happynefs of feeing
you he with another Gentleman
from *Canada* is gone for *Rhode Ifland*
in order for *Bofton* upon what Errant
I know not.

Capt *Smith* Mafter of the *Beaver*
defired me to acquaint your Excellency that he will fail the 20th of
this Inftant, I embrace the Opportunity to Exprefs my Concern for
the trouble my Father has given
you of his Letter and to affure your
Excellency I will not be wanting
to anfwer his defire fo far as I am
able, for I have nothing more at

heart than my tender Parent, and
the long life and profperity of your
Excellency and Family, being with
great truth and refpect

Sir
Your Excellencys
Moft humble and
moft obedient
Servant

Mr. Wileman to Mr. Bobin.

Sʳ

A S to any particular order or
minutes relating to any perfon's particular bufinefs, I hold it
requifite you may give copies of yᵉ
minutes or orders of Council. But
as to private affairs or yᵉ ftate of
yᵉ government without particular
order from yᵉ Governʳ and Councill I would not give copies of fuch.
I am Sʳ your humble fervt
H. W.

Aa

Isaac Bobin to Lewis Morris, Jun.

Sir

I DO not find that I am impow-
ered to give out any attefted
copys of the minutes of Councill
&ca relating to publick affairs, or
the affairs of the Government here,
without an order from the Board.
I am with refpeet Sir Your moft
obedient fervant

Is BOBIN

Lewis Morris Junr Efqr

Isaac Bobin to Lewis Morris, Jun.

Sir

I AM commanded by his Excellency to acquaint you that this
day he communicated to the Coun-

cil his Majefty's Warrant to him
difmiffing you from being one of
the members of that Board, a copy
whereof is inclofed. And I am
ordered by his Excellency to tell
you that purfuant to his Majefty's
Royal Will and pleafure, he has
difmift you from your place at that
Board and fworn and admitted
Phillip Cortlandt Efq^r in your room

I am

Sr

Your humble serv^t

Is BOBIN

To *Lewis Morris* Junr Efq.

Ifaac Bobin to George Clarke.

SECRETARY'S OFFICE, NEW YORK,

September the 14th 1730.

Hon^d Sir,

I RECEIVED yours of Saturday
laft by Mr *Corey* and now fend
by him the hatt for Mafter *Hyde*,

a p^d of Bohea Tea and a pound of Thread.

There has not been any Councill fince you left the Town, the Governour paft laft week very merrily but his Exc^y is now laid up with the gout.

All the Wills for Mr *Silvefter* are finifhed and delivered to Mr. *Corey*.

INDEX.

A*

B*

informed of rumors refpecting gov. Burnet and Mifs Vanhorn, 69 ; wants a fober man to teach his children, ib. ; informed that the N. Y. affembly is further prorogued, 74, 79 ; vifits New York, 76 ; his quarterly warrants fent to, 78 ; informed that the gov. returned to New York, but went to Amboy foon after, 78 ; fpeeches and addrefs at the N. J. affembly fent to, 80 ; news from England fent to, 81, 119, 126; letters from gov. Burnet fent to, 81 ; gov. Burnet requefts his prefence in New York, 83, 85 : informed that a committee has been appointed to examine the treafurer's accounts, 84, and that Mr. Philipfe has been removed from the council, 85 ; alfo, that the gov. is about to go to Albany, 88 ; return of the gov. from Albany announced to, 92 ; gov. Burnet informed that he is prevented by illnefs from waiting on his exc., 94 ; gov. B. receives the information in ominous filence, 95 ; is very craving for money, 96; bibles fent to, 97 ; his warrants figned, 104 ; informed that the gov. is expected from Amboy, and promifed fome fnuff, 105 ; informed of horfes which col. Rutfen has for fale, 106 ; defires to purchafe negroes, 109 (fee *Negroes*); report on the incidents of his office read in council, 109 ; council object to his falary being paid in preference to all others, 110 ; minutes of council on abftract of patents fent to, 111 ; fome members of the council ill difpofed towards, 113 ; informed that the gov. is going to N. Jerfey, 115, 182, and that his exc. declines appointing furrogates in remote counties, 119 ; a wig making for, 120; informed that the N. Y.

C*

pointment of gov. Burnet received at, 26; foldier
drowned at, ib. ; a fhark at, ib. ; negroes expected
from the Weft Indies at, 33, 36, 39 (fee *Negroes*);
gov. Burnet expected at, 35 ; a veffel arrives with
negroes from Barbadoes at, 36 ; H. M. fhip Kinfale fails from, 40 ; lotteries in, 43, 64, 70; no
Albany ftale beer in, 46; Mr. Clarke leaves, 51,
76 ; no marble tiles in, 53 ; news of the ruinous
fall of South Sea ftock received at, 56, 81 ; news
from England received at, 56, 81, 119, 121 ;
veffels arrived from England at, 56, 81, 119, 121,
137, 161, 165, 170 ; news of a probable peace
with Spain received at, 57 ; gov. Burnet about to
go to New Jerfey from, 62 ; death of col. Heathcote in, 64 ; lotteries in, 64, 70; much talk of
gov. Burnet and Mary Vanhorn in, 68 ; wet
weather in, 75 ; gov. Burnet arrives from Amboy
at, 78 ; great preparations for the marriage of
gov. Burnet making at, 80; Mr. Clarke requefted
by gov. Burnet to come to, 83 ; few members of
the council in town, 85; gov. Burnet about to
embark for Albany from, 88 ; fever and ague at,
89 ; general complaint of the dullnefs of trade at,
90; gov. Burnet returns from Albany to, 92 ;
Venice chalk all bought up by the ladies of, 97 ;
gov. Burnet expected from Amboy at, 105, and
about to go for Jerfey, 115, 125, 145, 182; veffel from Jamaica arrives at, 127; veffel from Barbadoes arrives at, 138 ; capt. Solgard, R. N., arrives with his fhip at, 139, 159, 187 ; confiderable damage done by a ftorm to the docks at, 141 ;
mayor and fheriff of, reappointed, 145 ; Mr.
Brownell fchoolmafter at, 150; no Lilly's gram-

E*

F*

ERRATA.

p. 49, l. 6 from top, *for* Pevice, *read*, Peirce.
p. 50, l. 12 from top, *for* Sonmine, *read*, Soumine.
p. 137, l. 3 from bottom, *after* here, *insert*, a sloop.